Water and Rural Communities

The overall theme of this book concerns the multiplicity and complexities of discursive constructions of water in Western economies in relation to irrigation communities. The authors argue that the politics of place is given meaning in relation to local knowledges and within multiple and multiscalar institutional frameworks involved with the social, physical, economic and political practices associated with water. They are particularly concerned with water at the local level, including how it is exchanged, managed and given meaning.

Using case studies from Australia and the United States of America, it is shown how water use and community relations, particularly during times of drought, are central to developing understandings about how communities challenge, adapt and respond to policy developments. The book also brings to light how unequal distribution of resources and risk conspicuously come to the surface during times of drought, illustrating that water is a political subject occupying a unique position, moving between the natural and social worlds.

Lia Bryant is an Associate Professor and Director of the Centre for Social Change in the School of Psychology, Social Work and Social Policy, University of South Australia.

Jodie George is a Researcher and Lecturer in the School of Communication, International Studies and Languages, University of South Australia.

Earthscan Studies in Water Resource Management

For more information and to view forthcoming titles in this series, please visit the Routledge website: www.routledge.com/books/series/ECWRM/

Transboundary Water Politics in the Developing World
By Naho Mirumachi

International Water Law and the Quest for Common Security
By Bjørn-Oliver Magsig

Water, Power and Identity
The Cultural Politics of Water in the Andes
By Rutgerd Boelens

Water and Cities in Latin America
Challenges for Sustainable Development
Edited by Ismael Aguilar-Barajas, Jürgen Mahlknecht, Jonathan Kaledin and Marianne Kjellén

Catchment and River Basin Management
Integrating Science and Governance
Edited by Laurence Smith, Keith Porter, Kevin M. Hiscock. Mary Jane Porter and David Benson

Transboundary Water Management and the Climate Change Debate
Anton Earle, Ana Elisa Cascão, Stina Hansson, Anders Jägerskog, Ashok Swain and Joakim Öjendal

Rules, Norms and NGO Advocacy Strategies
Hydropower Development on the Mekong River
Yumiko Yasuda

The Mekong: A Socio-legal Approach to River Basin Development
Ben Boer, Philip Hirsch, Fleur Johns, Ben Saul and Natalia Scurrah

Trans-jurisdictional Water Law and Governance
Edited by Janice Gray, Cameron Holley and Rosemary Rayfuse

Water and Rural Communities
Local Politics, Meaning and Place
Lia Bryant with Jodie George

Water and Rural Communities
Local politics, meaning and place

Lia Bryant
with Jodie George

First published 2016
by Routledge
2 Park Square, Milton Park, Abingdon, Oxon OX14 4RN

and by Routledge
711 Third Avenue, New York, NY 10017

Routledge is an imprint of the Taylor & Francis Group, an informa business

© 2016 Lia Bryant and Jodie George

The right of Lia Bryant and Jodie George to be identified as authors of this work has been asserted by them in accordance with sections 77 and 78 of the Copyright, Designs and Patents Act 1988.

All rights reserved. No part of this book may be reprinted or reproduced or utilised in any form or by any electronic, mechanical, or other means, now known or hereafter invented, including photocopying and recording, or in any information storage or retrieval system, without permission in writing from the publishers.

Trademark notice: Product or corporate names may be trademarks or registered trademarks, and are used only for identification and explanation without intent to infringe.

British Library Cataloguing-in-Publication Data
A catalogue record for this book is available from the British Library

Library of Congress Cataloging in Publication Data
Names: Bryant, Lia, author. | George, Jodie, author.
Title: Water and rural communities : local politics, meaning and place / Lia Bryant with Jodie George.
Description: London ; New York : Routledge, [2016] | Series: Earthscan studies in water resource management | Includes bibliographical references and index.
Identifiers: LCCN 2016005698| ISBN 9780415723589 (hbk) | ISBN 9781315857602 (ebk)
Subjects: LCSH: Water-supply--Political aspects--Australia--Renmark (S.A.) | Water-supply--Political aspects--California--Fresno. | Water rights--Australia--Renmark (S.A.) | Water rights--California--Fresno. | Irrigation farming--Political aspects--Australia--Renmark (S.A.) | Irrigation farming--Political aspects--California--Fresno. | Renmark (S.A.)--Politics and government. | Freson (Calif.)--Politics and government.
Classification: LCC HD1700.R46 B78 2016 | DDC 333.91009794/83--dc23
LC record available at https://lccn.loc.gov/2016005698

ISBN: 978-0-415-72358-9 (hbk)
ISBN: 978-1-315-85760-2 (ebk)

Typeset in Times
by Saxon Graphics Ltd, Derby

For Tim Bryant
For James and Janice Robar

Contents

List of figures ix
Acknowledgments xi

1 The poetics and politics of water and communities 1
2 Contextualising water policy in irrigation communities 23
3 Memory, place-making and water 41
4 Material sites/sights and spatialities of exclusion 60
5 Riskscapes 87
6 Community futures 112
7 Realms of knowing 133

Index 142

Figures

1.1	'Keep Saving CA' notice on a restaurant table	3
1.2	Valley farms protest, Central California	4
1.3	Map of Southeastern Australia showing the Murray–Darling Basin, the Riverland, and Renmark, South Australia	15
1.4	Map of California, USA, showing the location of Fresno and the Central Valley	16
4.1	Renmark Irrigation Trust building	69
4.2	Renmark Irrigation Trust boardroom	70
6.1	'Congress' flawed laws', Central California	121
6.2	'Politicians created the water crisis', Central California	122

Acknowledgments

Thank you to Dr Jodie George for authoring Chapters 2 and 3 and coauthoring Chapter 5 and for providing feedback and discussion in relation to the overall book.

Many thanks to Dr Kris Clarke for hosting us in Fresno and assisting us with accessing participants. Many thanks to the participants from the Riverland in South Australia, the Renmark Irrigation Trust, Australia and the participants from Central California, USA.

We acknowledge the *International Journal of Water Resources Development* for permission to use 'Bryant, L. and George, J., 2016. Examining uncertainty and trust among irrigators and regulatory bodies in the Murray-Darling basin. *International Journal of Water Resources Development,* 32(1), pp.102-115'.

Thank you to Dr Bridget Garnham for your assistance and support, to Katerina Bryant and Mathew Drogemuller for assistance with referencing and editing.

The South Australia data was collected as part of an Australian Research Council Grant and Central Californian data collection was funded by the University of South Australia.

1 The poetics and politics of water and communities

Water has been a subject of cultural thought and representation over centuries across diverse continents. It is used and represented in art, philosophy, religion and literature. Past and contemporary depictions and imaginaries of water, its surfaces and reflections, its depth and underworlds, have shaped ways of living with, and dreaming about, rivers, oceans, streams, rain, snow and ice. The Musée de L'Orangerie in Paris became one such place for dreaming when, after World War I, Monet donated to the state his canvases of lakes and water lilies in order to create a place of repose in a bustling city. These canvases continue to fill the curvaceous walls of the museum, reminding of us of gentle and lavish waves, and as such capture common metaphoric meanings of water as renewing, calming and cleansing. There are also many compelling examples of water, art and depictions of human and non-human well-being found in past and contemporary Australian Indigenous art. Paintings on rock and canvas hold cultural stories, which are woven into images of place, with the most recurring being spiral lines representing running water, circular forms recording the presence of water holes and Rainbow Serpents who reside in waterholes to regenerate land. Together these depictions form a map but also a spiritual place – a story of the dreaming.

These artistic constructions of water speak to place-based meanings and show interstices between elements, place and subjects (Macauley, 2006, p. 188). In this way, water, as an important aspect of nature, is more than a natural resource but is inescapably social; thus concepts like 'social natures' or 'social/cultural and material natures' assist us to recognise the ways in which environment and culture are intertwined as relational actants (Castree and Braun, 2001, p. 10). It is in this nexus between the social, historical, political, cultural and the material that this book positions its point of enquiry to examine water use and allocation at the local level in times of drought and water scarcity. At the forefront of this enquiry is an interrogation of the politics of place in irrigation communities to decipher knowledges, discursive meanings and practices that give rise to how water is governed, accessed, and its impact on livelihood and well-being. This book demonstrates that questions of social justice and unequal distribution of resources and risk conspicuously come to the surface during times of drought. It illustrates that water is a political subject occupying a unique position, moving between the natural and social worlds.

Through two case studies we empirically examine the dynamics of water access and use in irrigation communities during drought. The case studies provide a platform from which to understand the mutuality of water and community in and beyond the study sites, illustrating the historic, sociopolitical and material contexts, conditions, understandings and practices that shape both community and water use. The first case study is of the Riverland in South Australia, specifically the district of Renmark; and the second site is Central California, in particular the areas outlying and including Fresno. The Riverland experienced drought according to the official government definition of drought, which is a state determination of ongoing rainfall deficiency resulting in limited storage levels of water impacting on the ability to continue 'normal farming practices' (ABS, 2004). Drought was declared in the Riverland from 2001 to 2011. As the drought in the Riverland broke in 2011, California entered into drought conditions and remains so, with Governor Jerry Brown declaring California a drought State of Emergency in 2015. In the USA a drought is defined as:

> a period of drier-than-normal conditions that results in water-related problems. When rainfall is less than normal for several weeks, months, or years, the flow of streams and rivers declines, water levels in lakes and reservoirs fall, and the depth to water in wells increases. If dry weather persists and water-supply problems develop, the dry period can become a drought.
>
> (USDA, 2012, p. 4)

For the first time in many years, in both Australia and the USA, water scarcity extended to cities. Drought was no longer a 'farming problem' but surfaced into the consciousness of city dwellers as water use was increasingly rationed for household and business use in cities like Los Angeles and Adelaide.

Australia and the USA developed marketing campaigns to reduce household water consumption. Advertising on Australian television aimed to inspire 'good citizenship' through water saving. Citizens were reminded to not leave the tap on when brushing their teeth, to water their gardens at night and on alternate nights. By taking these measures the government assured the community we would 'Save the Murray–Darling Basin' for our children's future. South Australians also paid a levy to restore the river's health. California launched its 'Save Our Water Campaign' with household tips for saving water and rebates for householders who removed turf from their gardens. The impact of water scarcity in cities provided the context in which

Water and communities: poetics and politics 3

Figure 1.1 'Keep Saving CA' notice on a restaurant table

farming, mining and business practices and their water use was brought to the fore in the printed, electronic and social media. A recent story in the *New Yorker* with a headline asking 'Who's to blame for California's drought?' (Vara, April 8, 2015) encapsulates the moral discourses of citizenship and water use circulating in the USA and competing claims to water. As increasing numbers of people across rural and city borders are affected by drought, national consciousness about water use has become prevalent.

4 *Water and communities: poetics and politics*

For irrigators, drought has meant uncertain water allocations and therefore uncertainty associated with yields, feed for animals, and business and farm household income. In each site during drought there have been annual rulings about water allocation for agricultural use, causing contestation and friction within and across communities. In Australia these have resulted in protests during national consultative forums with the state about water legislation and contestations among Australian states located up and down the Murray–Darling Basin for 'just' water access. In the United States contestations over water allocation have resulted in litigious action from irrigators claiming their 'right' to water (see Chapters 2 and 5). These moral claims to water are framed within individualised rights-based discourses that focus on water as a private right (see Chapters 2, 4 and 5).

Understandings about water use, rights and allocations shape water-based practices and politics in irrigation communities. However, water and the rivers from which people draw their livelihood are enmeshed in place, and therefore also shape identities, belonging, memories and experience. In other words, meanings about water are also interconnected with meanings about community. We argue in Chapter 4 that questions of belonging are embedded in both historic and contemporary discourses and practices about water and place that emerge from the historic developments of different regions (see Chapter 2), the local water trusts (see Chapters 2 and 4), and the

Figure 1.2 Valley farms protest, Central California

social relations of production which are constituted from colonial narratives of the 'other', thereby excluding women, Indigenous peoples and diverse ethnic populations (see Chapter 4). These positions are continually re-enacted, and what we aim to do in this book is 'to evoke place as meeting place rather than as always already coherent, as open rather than bounded, as an ongoing production rather than pre-given' (Massey, 2006, p. 34). But place is not unlocated, that is, place has ongoing laws and established historical narratives, norms and memories which are not necessarily coherent or cohesive.

Massey's (2006) notion of place as porous is a vivid way to analyse river systems which flow across political and community borders and are thereby networked beyond the local to other places, impacting on the interstices between national and local politics. Thus, we also examine how the local communities which provide the sites of analysis are networked beyond local borders. Together, these case studies provide an international perspective from colonised nations through which to examine the complexities operating within rural communities whose existence relies, at least in part, on irrigation practices which are themselves multiscalar and contested.

In order to explicate the complex geopolitics of water we draw on landscape theories. However, despite a rich theorising on the subject of landscape, sociological and critical geographies have remained on the margins when examining the multiplicity and complexities of discursive constructions and embodied practices of water in rural economies. Much of what we know about water and rurality is focused on economics, law and the physical geography of water. These bodies of literature are concerned with water pollution, conservation, legislative frameworks and technological infrastructure (e.g. Boelens et al., 2010; Franks, 2000; Prosser, 2011). The social has been addressed in part, within the field of gender and development and specifically, water and Indigenous knowledges and practices (e.g. Bakker, 2010; Feldman, 2012; Rodríguez, 2006; Strang, 2004). It is now timely to turn to insights from sociology and critical geography to examine how river water is consumed, allocated and contested, in rural irrigation communities especially, to understand questions of power, justice and social inclusion/exclusion.

From landscapes to land/waterscapes

There is a long history of theorising about landscapes and a diverse body of work concerned with understanding what constitutes landscape (Matless, 2003; Wylie, 2007). Whilst the word 'landscape' anchors us to land and privileges land over water, sky and air, it has been constructed to mean more than land. Ostensibly, conceptualisations of landscape can be placed into four broad categories: landscape as an external phenomenon;

representations of landscape; landscape as entwined with subjectivities, and non-representational theories.

Across these spheres of knowledges meanings overlap and divisions are arbitrary; however, through these lenses we can trace the development of theorisations of landscape to understand how humans and non/humans interact, shape and create both landscapes and subjects. These knowledges provide a springboard from which to analyse land and waterscapes.

Landscapes from objective physicality to representation

The earliest ideas about landscapes proposed that they were external to subjects, to be viewed and described. Sauer (1963), a critical contributor to the external phenomenon view of landscapes, focused on landscape as an objective physical space (almost always rural) from which academics and artists could describe and draw conclusions. This has been an enduring and powerful conceptualisation, as it has often been the foundation for shaping future theorisations and critiques about landscapes as objective and static. During the cultural turn in geography in the 1980s and 1990s, landscape as an objective physical presence unrelated to culture was critiqued. New theorisations focused on understanding how depictions of landscapes and uses of landscapes represented cultural and historic meanings (Ingold, 1993; Cosgrove, 1998). Landscape in this school of thought was read as text and as such was open to interpretation. As Wylie (2007, p. 55, emphasis in original) suggests:

> in many of the cultural geographies ... landscape is quite closely identified with *landscape art*, a complex and diverse artistic genre evolving from the fifteenth century to the present day, and associated in particular with the visualisation of relationships between culture and nature. As a system for producing and transmitting meaning through visual symbols and representations, landscape art alongside cognate arts such as cartography, photography, poetry and literature, is a key medium through which Western and in particular European cultures have historically understood themselves, and their relations with other cultures and the natural world.

Representational understandings of landscapes sought to interpret the power relations inherent in and shaping landscapes. Cultural Marxists drew attention to the ordering and control of landscape for production (Lyson, 2006; Goodwin, 2006). Feminist scholars theorised landscapes as gendered spatialities reflecting on the public/private division of home and work as masculine and feminine spheres, demonstrating how some spaces become gendered and sexualised (e.g. bars, night spaces) (Bondi, 1993; Domosh, 1996). Feminist geographers invoking Haraway's politics of location (1988) also challenged how landscapes were viewed, bringing attention to situated embodiment. Situated embodiment refers to how subjects read and engage with space and produce knowledge. Hence, knowledge claims are historical, socio-political and subjective, shaped by gendered, classed, racialised and sexualised bodies also constituted in the context of age, ethnicity and (dis) ability. Rose (1993) and other social geographers (Bondi, 1993; Domosh, 1996) have shown how what is seen, noted and valued in a landscape is often from the perspective of the male gaze. In general, white men have described and theorised the social world, resulting in a universalising story of social history and an exclusion of multiple voices, a colonising of the voices of the most marginalised and a privileging of the white, middle-class male gaze. These interpretations brought a greater focus on power but as Wiley (2007, p. 92) states, 'The distinctive gradient of "new" cultural geographies, however, lay in the ascending status they accorded to representation and representational practices. This gradient may be witnessed substantively, methodologically and theoretically.' In this way, meanings of landscape shifted from the physical to the visual and textual with analyses of power emerging from representations and interpretation.

Relationality of nature and culture

Building on feminist theorising, which located situated knowledge and the gaze as crucial to how landscapes are read and understood, cultural and social geographers examined the ways in which landscapes and subjectivities intersected. The focus shifted to a more nuanced account of how culture and nature were relational (Ingold, 2000). One such relational aspect of nature and the social is the ways we profess to 'know' and organise nature through socio-historic, ideological and political processes. In this way, water may be understood also as a constructed entity whose presence and absence is embodied and complex, affecting and being affected by the daily movements of culture and political positioning. This is a generative view of ongoing human/non-human engagement where both nature and humans have actant potential. Here nature or environment is not conceived of as reductive, inert. Instead nature is changed and changing, and is 'simultaneously the subject and object' of landscape (Wiley, 2007, p. 159). Common understandings of nature evident in the reporting of news and in popular books have shown nature as ever changing, drawing on threats like floods, droughts, hurricanes, erupting volcanoes and earthquakes. As Massey (2006, p. 38) suggests, popular stories of nature show nature on the move, 'endlessly mobile, restless, given to violence and unpredictability ... never still, nor simply in balance'. Changes to nature, however, are not always so acutely dramatic and are also actant in their evolution over time, for example, in the formations of mountains and the migration and erosion of rocks. In relation to water both across and within land/waterscapes, the precipitation in space and time is uneven and rates of evaporation vary. As such, over time river water will ebb and flow.

The conceptualisation of the temporality of landscape (Bender, 2002) has been given particular attention within non-representational theories, which emerged in social geography in the early 2000s. A focus on temporality and landscape involved a revisiting and analysis of the past with an inclusion of the present and future by 'counter[ing] the impression so often left, that the present is some kind of achieved terminus' (Massey, 2006, p. 42). In this book, we trace temporal water flows and also the politics around access and use of water, which shift and change as water flows diminish or increase. We examine how settlement, statutory legislation and past and present governance practices shape how water is accessed: its quantity, for what purpose and by whom. Thus, by bringing into focus legislation and irrigation experiences over time, we show that the past is not simply reducible to memory (Hinchliffe, 2003), but is continuous. As Massey (2006, p. 46) so aptly states, 'landscape could be imagined as provisionally intertwined simultaneities of ongoing, unfinished stories' (see Chapter 3).

Non-representational theories have also underscored the interstices between landscape and the lived body – bodily practice, experience and performance in relation to nature. Hence, a range of empirical studies have emerged which examine the body and nature, focusing on outdoor recreational pursuits and nature as therapeutic (Brandth and Haugen, 2006; Crouch, 2006; Edensor, 2006). By walking in forests, swimming in rivers or gazing at hills, our bodies and minds experience place emotionally and sensuously (Tilley, 2004). In this way, subjectivities are constituted in relation to, as Whatmore states (2006, p. 603), inner life worlds 'co-fabricated between more-than-human bodies and a lively earth'. In regard to water and subjectivity, rivers in areas like the Riverland in South Australia are enmeshed in regional and personal identity. The river shapes what it means to belong in this landscape at multiple and intersecting emotional and embodied levels, that is, in terms of production, consumption, recreation and by the absorption of sensory responses to its sheer presence. How subjects come to 'be' within landscapes and what belonging means is, however, complicated by a politics of identity (Tilley, 2006). Tilley (2006, p. 15) argues:

> What kinds of landscape and place we produce, and want, are inextricably bound up with the politics of identity, for ideas about both relate to whom we want to live with and whom we want to exclude, who belongs and who does not, to issues of class, ethnicity, gender and sexuality.

Power relations built on dominance and resistance circulate around ownership of land and by default water, equally shaping subjectivities and relations to rivers. In this book we will show the diversity and contestations around subjectivities and landscape, especially in relation to frontier imaginaries (Prout and Howitt, 2009) which shape human engagement with land and water as well as subjectivities, emotions, health, knowledges and working bodies. In this way, rivers and landscapes are perceived and sensed, materially contested and embodied through work, health, emotions and the senses.

Local and global

Reiterating Massey's point that landscapes are meeting places, it is important to consider how the politics of belonging and activity in the river communities, which are the focus of this book, extend beyond national borders. There has been much debate about what terms should be used to understand flows and disconnects beyond nation states. The term globalisation, which has been in use for some time, has been critiqued for dichotomising the local and the global, focusing on what happens outside of nation states and constructing the local as a victim of global economic forces (Robinson, 2011). In attempts to avoid binary thinking and to intersect the economic and cultural, and show that the global and the local 'infiltrate each other' (Blackwood, 2005, p. 221), some theorists have favoured the term 'transnational' (e.g. Brickell and Datta, 2011; Ong, 1999; Grewal and Kaplan, 2001; Bachetta, 2002). As Binnie (2004, p. 34) has argued, the term 'transnational' does, however, centralise 'the resilience of the nation state'. In terms of local ruralities, Askins (2009, p. 366) suggests the concept 'transrurality' is a useful conceptualisation of rurality that:

> encapsulates the specificities of place and is open to mobility and desire – in order to displace rural ... as only an exclusionary white space and reposition it as a site within muticultural, multiethnic, transnational and mobile social imaginaries.

Whilst these debates are ongoing and any 'form of categorisation both opens and restricts understandings' (Gorman-Murray et al., 2013, p. 228), we find the term 'transrurality' helpful in relation to theorising land/waterscapes in river communities. It enables a distancing from transnational discourse, it emphasises multiscalar movements and allows for the 'interpenetration of economic, cultural, political and affective structures and experiences' (Gorman-Murray et al., 2013, p. 228).

One of the first points of transrurality evident in the story of our river communities is the establishment of irrigation channels for production. The Canadian born Chaffey brothers, William, George and Charles, who were engineers and irrigation planners, developed irrigation systems in both California and Renmark toward the end of the nineteenth century. As explored in Chapters 2 and 4, irrigation knowledge and professional engineering practice was very much a global process, a brotherhood of expertise to build empire and nation (Zwarteveen, 2008). Settler and frontier imaginaries have denied Indigenous ownership of land and 'point to the selective and frequently hegemonic meanings of rural life and environments based on agrarian populations, private property and White histories and highly managed nature-society relations' (Panelli et al., 2009, p. 357). Each transrurality is deeply tied to flows of migration, both national and global, occurring from colonial pasts but also through successive waves of migration and temporary migrations of seasonal workers (Nelson, 2008).

Hence, while there are local flavours, conditions and contexts to power relations, there are globalising processes. Similarly, rivers also flow within and across geographical and political borders. Power relations are tied to national identity politics and policies about water and the economy, as well as relations with other states within nations, global corporations and commodity markets. It is these complex forces and how they are interpreted and reinterpreted at the local level which we aim to examine in relation to water allocation and use. As Bakker (2003, p. 49) argues, 'water circulation, in short, is dependant upon institutions and practices as much as on the hydrological cycle, it is not only physically produced, but also socially enacted'. This social enactment is underpinned by contested knowledges. Critical to uncovering the multiple and shifting contexts, conditions and practices of water within transrural places are competing knowledge regimes about climate change; agrarian discourses of moral worth about producing food for the nation (Bryant and Garnham, 2015); Indigenous knowledges (Nikolakis and Grafton, 2014; Wirf et al., 2008); professional and academic knowledges (Buizer et al., 2011; Zwarteveen, 2008); and so forth.

Land/waterscapes

Uncovering knowledges about water is crucial to understanding land/waterscapes. Linton (2010) has posed the simple but complex question: What is water? He argues that 'We give to water that which enables it to realise its potential ... we mix language, gods, bodies, and thought with water to produce the worlds and the selves we inhabit' (Linton, 2010, p. 4). At the same time, however, hegemonic discourses about water exist, drawn from Western knowledges that produce the idea that water is an abstraction removed from political-social ways of living. Linton goes on to argue (2010, p. 5) that water is:

> primarily a process rather than a thing. The 'water process' is that out of which every specific instance of water gets abstracted, including scientific representations such as H_2O. On this view, things such as H_2O do not constitute the fundamental reality of water but, rather, are fixations that

occur at the nexus of the water process and the social process of producing and representing scientific knowledge.

What has been made known through scientific knowledge and in particular Horton's hydrological cycle, is how water has been made calculable and as such a resource, a product of scarcity or abundance (Linton, 2010). As hegemonic meanings about water are constituted in relation to power and privilege, discourses of water scarcity, as we show in Chapter 5, are constituted and 'fixed in any particular time and place [and] can therefore be seen as a function of the relative power of different social actors' (Linton, 2010, p. 13). It is this shaping of water as a political product and entity flowing through socio-natural worlds in which this book seeks to understand interstices between community and water.

Consequently, '[for Linton] water becomes what it is in relation to other things and processes; it is what we make of it' (Wynne, 2010, p. xv). If 'water is what we make of it' then social and cultural geography until recently have made little of water. Over the past decade there has been growth in the field of 'wet geographies', beginning with Steinberg's conceptualisation of the maritime world in 1999 and a subsequent surge of scholarship focusing on understanding the socio-nature of water (e.g. Anderson and Peters, 2014; Linton, 2010; Vannini and Taggart, 2014). Steinberg's (1999; 2014) work challenged geography's landlocked notion of landscape, arguing that oceans constitute 70 per cent of the planet's surface. This 70 per cent of oceans, however, has been conceived of as the 'other' to land and conceptually located within a land/sea binary. Increasingly, scholars have demonstrated that the sea is spatially connected to other spaces and places and as such is open and converges with such spaces. Anderson and Peters (2014, p. 6), also focusing on oceans, have argued that

> oceans and seas are recognised as equally fundamental within processes of social-cultural, political and economic transformation, rather than acting merely as conceptual devices for understanding these processes.

Steinberg's (2001) work in particular has drawn attention to how societies use and engage with oceans in relation to fishing, trade, war and other practices. Others have also given attention to non-human actors like fish, insects and so on (Bear and Eden, 2011; Probyn, 2014), shaping waterscapes and human engagement in waterscapes.

In challenging the centring of terra in conceptualisations of landscape, Vannini and Taggart (2014, p. 98) have asked:

> What would happen if we instead viewed the land from the perspective of water? What would happen if we wanted to see similarities and overlaps between land and water, rather than distinctions and boundaries?

These provocative questions open up the possibilities for reading landscapes as land/waterscapes and suggests there is room for 'extending the idea of the hybrid environments beyond not just a culture-nature binary but beyond the deeply entrenched water-land dichotomy' (Lahiri-Dutt, 2014, p. 507). Lahiri-Dutt's (2014) central thesis is that there is no dividing line between land and water. Water, while theoretically understood as apart from land, may also blend with land in certain ways:

> *sometimes a given environment, sometimes another, sometimes both and sometimes neither.* The blend of water/lands is such that the environment is continually in flux, not a mixture of this and that.
> (Lahiri-Dutt, 2014, p. 522, emphasis in original)

The Bengal flood plains are used as an example where land becomes saturated by water and is neither water nor land, but at times both. Drought is another such example where dry riverbeds are also hybrid spaces, neither land nor water, sometimes one and sometimes both.

While Lahiri-Dutt's (2014) focus is on hybrid environments, removing the boundaries between land and water opens up the possibility for theorising about the interstices between land and water and reframing landscapes as water/landscapes.

Finally, Tilley's (2006) summarising of Barbara Bender's (2002; 2006) work brings us acutely to where we are now in land/waterscape theorising – an academic space of diversity and becoming. As Tilley (2006, pp. 7–8) states:

> landscapes are contested, worked and re-worked by people according to particular individual, social and political circumstances. As such they are always in process, rather than static, being and becoming. Landscapes are on the move ... [shaped by] disasporas ... identity[ies], people making homes in new places, landscapes are structures of feeling, palimpsests of past and present, outcomes of social practice, products of colonial and post-colonial identities and the western gaze ... They get actively reworked, interpreted and understood in relation to differing social and political agendas, forms of social memory and biographically become sensuously embodied in a multitude of ways.

In relation to theorising land/waterscapes throughout this book we will pick up on many of these strands of thought, and in particular: the ways in which water is used differently within communities for production, thereby changing land/waterscapes (see Chapters 2 and 5); contested knowledges around water use (see Chapters 4, 6 and 7); colonial assumptions and practices about land and water that shape present day governance (see Chapter 4); politics associated with water rights and access (see Chapters 2, 5 and 6); and social memory and biography which gives meanings to lives lived in and around rivers (see Chapters 3 and 6).

Methodology

The case studies used in this book stem from two distinct but interrelated empirical studies. The first was funded by an Australian Research Council Linkage Grant (2010–2012) and focused on understandings of changing water legislation by irrigators. It also explored water practices, discourses and meanings about water allocation, scarcity and the river and questions of social inclusion and exclusion in water politics. Semi-structured interviews were held with twenty-four irrigators, most of whom were male, aged between 35 and 80, from Renmark, South Australia. These irrigators belonged to the Renmark Irrigation Trust (RIT), the governing water trust in the district. The sample included new RIT members (joined between 2007 and 2010) and longer-term members (more than fifteen years). Irrigators came from a mix of property sizes consistent with the distribution within the RIT (25 per cent < 2 hectares [ha]; 25 per cent 2–5 ha; 25 per cent 5–10 ha; 25 per cent > 10 ha[1]) and grew predominantly wine grapes, almonds, stone fruit, citrus and horticulture. The sample also included six key stakeholders and community members including representation from local government, water governing bodies, the secondary school, and local business and commodity groups (see Bryant and George, 2016). The second study, funded by the University of South Australia and conducted in 2013, was held in the USA and involved semi-structured interviews with twelve participants, all male, and included those representing water governing bodies, activists, irrigators and journalists. The sample was drawn mostly from Central California and in particular Fresno and its surrounds. Academic colleagues from the USA assisted us to identify interviewees, which then enabled snowballing to build the sample according to diversity associated with official roles, work responsibilities and potential attitudes in relation to water allocation and use. The two study sites were chosen to provide an analysis of contexts and conditions of drought and water allocation at the local level. These communities share some commonalities in relation to climatic conditions and crops produced; and are colonised nations with distinct histories, and legislative and cultural differences. As such, the studies provide a temporal picture of drought and transruralities, enabling us to identify some of the contexts and conditions that shape water politics in these colonised, frontier, settler countries. As scholars like Zwarteveen (2008) and others (e.g. Laurie, 2005; Sultana, 2009) have demonstrated, colonisation, irrigation, water governance and politics remain primarily a male province. Our case studies show that histories and contemporary practices and discourses about water remain dominated by men (see Chapter 5).

Questions asked of both samples stemmed from the following topics: meanings associated with place and water and in particular the meanings about the function of the principal rivers; interpretations of water politics at local and global scales; equity in relation to water access; current legislation; and future hopes for their communities. Interviews were audio-recorded, transcribed and analysed using a thematic analysis (Neuman, 2012). Texts were read to seek patterns and differences across transcripts and key themes were summarised and tested within each study data set and where appropriate across the whole data set. Data extracts were therefore purposefully selected (Patton, 2002) from across the two data sets to examine narratives, intersections and disjunctures. The analyses that emerge in this book occur from writing and analysis as inseparable activities. As Bryant and Garnham (2015) explain, data comes to life in the context of writing:

> The analysis … was coincidental and inseparable from writing and does not therefore exist independent from … writing. In her co-authored chapter with Richardson, St Pierre (2005: 967 emphasis in original) exhorts the reader to think along with Richardson that 'writing *is* thinking, writing *is* analysis, writing is indeed a seductive and tangled *method* of discovery'. In this sense, St Pierre (2005: 969), citing her own work, suggests that writing as a method of inquiry is 'a condition of possibility for "producing different knowledge and producing knowledge differently"'.

The Riverland

The RIT is situated in the town of Renmark, which is in the Riverland, South Australia (see Figure 1.3).

The Riverland is a major South Australian fruit-growing region of state, national and international significance, producing one quarter of Australia's wine grapes and 30 per cent of its citrus fruit (Pink, 2008); the current estimated value of agricultural production for the region is AU$777.3 million (Riverland Councils, 2012). Irrigation involves authorised access to extract water from rivers or bores, and half to two thirds of all farms in the Riverland are irrigated properties (Pink, 2008). The amount of water available for irrigation in Australia varies per year depending on rain and water storage and allocations required for environmental, agricultural and urban needs. Approximately 80 per cent of all water used in South Australia is applied to irrigated crops, with 40 per cent supplied by the River Murray, which forms part of the Murray–Darling Basin, containing the country's three longest rivers: the Darling (2,740 km), the Murray (2,530 km) and the Murrumbidgee (1,690 km).

However, this region and its capacity for irrigation are under threat. Average annual temperatures have increased by 0.9°C since 1910, with most

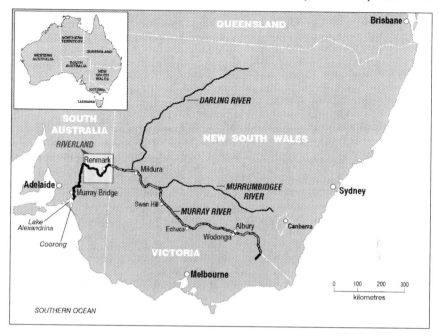

Figure 1.3 Map of Southeastern Australia showing the Murray–Darling Basin, the Riverland, and Renmark, South Australia

Source: Carto Graphics (Unley, South Australia), 2015.

of this warming occurring since 1950, and much of eastern and southwestern Australia has become drier (Department of Agriculture, Fisheries and Forestry, 2008). This has contributed to historically low river flows in the country's largest river system, the Murray–Darling Basin (MDB), with run-off in the decade between 1997 and 2006 up to 50 per cent lower than the long-term mean in the southernmost parts of the MDB in the state of South Australia (CSIRO, 2009). In 2010, total water storage in the MBD was at 26.1 per cent capacity and rose to 80.8 per cent capacity in 2011 with the breaking of the drought (Department of Sustainability, Environment, Water Populations and Communities, 2011). Specific challenges to irrigation resulting from these environmental changes were significant, including an increased need for environmental management and water use efficiency, and a greater fragmentation of the agricultural industry due to increasing competition for access to water (*Australian Natural Resources Atlas* – Department of Environment, n.d.). Typified by small landholdings called 'blocks', the Riverland region in particular has experienced significant change as a consequence of these drought conditions, the chronic over-allocation of water, radical changes in local climates, and agricultural structural adjustment.

Site 2

Fresno is situated in Central California (see Figure 1.4).

The Fresno Irrigation District was formed in 1920 under the California Irrigation Districts Act, creating a public oversight body by purchasing over 800 miles of canals and distribution works from the privately owned Fresno Canal and Land Company for $1.75 million (Fresno Irrigation District, 2015). Most of Fresno County is part of the Tulare Lake Hydrologic Region, the largest agricultural region in California (Brown et al., 2014, p. TL-11), with an average annual rainfall of only 29 cm since 1985, less than half of the average of California, and 71 per cent less than the national average (WeatherDB, 2015). As a result, like many communities with such limited precipitation, Fresno's primary source of water is groundwater. Across the district, approximately 500,000 acre-feet of water is delivered annually to agricultural users, supplemented by entitlements from Kings River, though these allocations continue to decline as greater supplies are needed to ensure the

Figure 1.4 Map of California, USA, showing the location of Fresno and the Central Valley
Source: Carto Graphics (Unley, South Australia), 2015.

stability of the groundwater table for urban use (Fresno Irrigation District, 2015). Irrigation is drawn largely from Kings River and the major water courses include the San Joaquin, Delta-Mendota Canal, Big Creek, Friant Kern Canal, Helm Canal and Madera Canal. It is one of the largest, most diverse agricultural areas in the USA and withdraws more ground water than other USA counties. The Kings River is approximately 201 kilometres long and divides along the San Joaquin Valley into the North Fork Distributary, South Fork Distributary and Clark's Fork Distributary. The North Fork Distributary connects to Fresno South and drains into the San Joaquin River. The Kings River provides water to fourteen Central Valley cities. While there is some discrepancy in figures associated with Kings River water flow, it has been expected in 2015 to be between 4,000 and 6,000 cubic feet per second. In comparison, in 2011 river flows at their highest were approximately within 21,130 cubic feet per second.

Fresno produces diverse crops, and its main products include horticulture, almonds, oranges and grapes, as well as poultry, cattle and dairy cattle. Fresno contributes approximately US$5.6 billion to the national economy (Census of Agriculture, United States Department of Agriculture, 2012). In 2012 there were approximately 5,683 farms covering approximately 1.88 million acres, which together generated more than US$7 billion in 2014, an increase of 9.26 per cent from the previous year despite the impact of drought conditions (County of Fresno, 2014). The average agricultural landholding is approximately 300 acres, though family farms may range in size from less than 10 acres to 25,000 acres (United States Department of Agriculture, 2012). Despite this economic growth, the severity of the drought, the overdraft of groundwater, and the degradation of key infrastructure present serious challenges to the sustainability of agriculture within the region (Hanak et al., 2011).

Overview of the book

The book consists of seven chapters. We begin by providing the historical, policy, legislative and political context in which water is made available for irrigation in the two study sites in Australia and the United States of America (see Chapter 2). We examine histories of shifting water policies and governance and how these are brought into the present to frame irrigation practices. Chapter 3 examines memory and placemaking, specifically focusing on the narratives of irrigators to gain insights into how water and community are constituted over time. In this chapter we explore how memory is a significant device used in creating the contours of irrigation communities. We trace shifting knowledges and meanings about the availability and use of water to identify how drought may disrupt or reconfigure community.

Chapter 4 focuses on the Riverland alone, and examines the material sites that shape irrigation communities and water governance at the local level. This chapter brings the material into focus in relation to buildings and furnishings to examine how settlement and community come into being in communities established primarily as irrigation communities. In particular, the chapter uses as its site of analysis the historical building of the Renmark Irrigation Trust to make visible how contemporary contestations and meaning making about water intersect with the politics of location and the globally interconnectedness of place. We explore how materiality and memory shape imaginaries and experiences of place, constituting and reconstituting practices of inclusion/exclusion whereby Indigenous peoples, women and ethnically diverse groups are often excluded from water governance. We demonstrate that the human-made material world is a critical interpretive tool to understand power relations in irrigation communities.

In the next chapter (Chapter 5), we take up the question of drought in relation to local responses, conditions and contexts to understand how drought is lived in irrigation communities. The politics of drought are enmeshed within the interstices of socio-cultural natures, shaping land/waterscapes into riskscapes. This chapter centralises risk to examine relations of risk, multiple meanings of risk and the unequal distribution of risks. Hence, Chapter 5 seeks to understand how risks are revealed, mediated, managed, contested and lived.

Chapter 6 examines community futures, for the Riverland post-drought and for Central California during drought. Temporality is used to explore the community time–space dynamic to reveal the possible futures for irrigation communities. In this chapter we argue that historical connections inscribed in legislation, past water practices and embodied biographies shape the present and possible futures of irrigation communities. As such, futures come into being through the folding and unfolding of the past into the present. The chapter shows that the possible conditions which give rise to the futures of irrigation communities are closely tied to the way irrigators discursively, performatively and in practice align water to individual rights. A rights-based discourse is mobilised to protect the perceived threat and risk to water allocations. Collective action, whilst always somewhat fractured, is used to resist and shape policy and change and configure community futures.

The final chapter of the book we have entitled 'Realms of Knowing' as 'knowledges' and 'knowing' weave through the text informing virtually all aspects of land/waterscapes in irrigation communities. We explore tacit and articulated knowledges shaping both water and community that speak to settlement, drought, inclusion, identities, economies and water governance and practices. Such knowledges are hegemonic, disparate, contested and fragmented realms of knowing which are recalled through memories, discourses, embodied practices and cultures. They shape the theatre of water politics and thus, irrigation communities.

Note

1 Acres are used as a land measurement in the USA. One acre equals 0.0015625 square miles, 4,840 square yards, 43,560 square feet and 4,047 square metres and an acre is equivalent to 0.405 hectares. In Australia the hectare is used: one hectare contains about 2.47 acres.

References

Anderson, J. and Peters, K., eds, 2014. *Water worlds: human geographies of the ocean*. Surrey: Ashgate Publishing.
Askins, K., 2009. Crossing divides: ethnicity and rurality. *Journal of Rural Studies*, 25, pp. 365–375.
Australian Bureau of Statistics, 2004. *Year book Australia, 2004: environment*. Available at: www.abs.gov.au/ausstats/abs@.nsf/0/6289FC8086876C0CCA256 DEA00053931?opendocument (Accessed 18 November 2015).
Bacchetta, P., 2002. Rescaling transnational 'queerdom': lesbian and 'lesbian' identitary–positionalities in Delhi in the 1980s. *Antipode*, 34(5), pp. 947–973.
Bakker, K., 2003. *An uncooperative commodity: privatizing water in England and Wales*. Oxford: Oxford University Press.
Bakker, K., 2010. *Privatizing water: governance failure and the world's urban water crisis*. Ithaca, NY: Cornell University Press.
Bear, C. and Eden, S., 2011. Thinking like a fish? Engaging with nonhuman difference through recreational angling. *Environment and Planning D*, 29(2), pp. 336–352.
Bender, B., 2002. Time and landscape. *Current Anthropology*, 43(4), pp. 103–112.
Bender, B., 2006. Place and landscape. In: C. Tilley, W. Keane, S. Küchler, M. Rowlands and P. Spyer, eds, *Handbook of material culture*. London: Sage, pp. 303–314.
Binnie, J., 2004. *The globalisation of sexuality*. London: Sage.
Blackwood, E., 2005. Transnational sexualities in one place: Indonesian readings. *Gender and Society*, 19(2), pp. 221–242.
Boelens, R., Getchens, D. and Guevara, G.I., eds, 2010. *Out of the mainstream: water rights, politics and identity*. London: Earthscan.
Bondi, L., 1993. Locating identity politics. In: M. Keith and S. Pile, eds, *Place and the politics of identity*. London: Routledge, pp. 84–101.
Brandth, B. and Haugen, M., 2006. Doing rural masculinity – from logging to outfield tourism. *Journal of Gender Studies*, 14(1), pp. 13–22.
Brickell, K. and Datta, A., eds, 2011. *Translocal geographies*. Surrey: Ashgate Publishing.
Brown Jr, E.G., Laird, J. and Cowin, N., 2014. *California water plan: investing in innovation and infrastructure. Volume 2: regional reports*. California: Department of Water Resources.
Bryant, L. and Garnham, B., 2015. The fallen hero: masculinity, shame and farmer suicide in Australia. *Gender, Place and Culture*, 22(1), pp. 67–82.
Bryant, L. and George, J., 2016. Examining uncertainty and trust among irrigators and regulatory bodies in the Murray–Darling basin. *International Journal of Water Resources Development*, 32(1), pp. 102–115.

Buizer, M., Arts, B. and Kok, K., 2011. Governance, scale and the environment: the importance of recognizing knowledge claims in transdisciplinary areas. *Ecology and Society*, 16(1), p. 21. Online. www.ecologyandsociety.org/vol16/iss1/art21/

Castree, N. and Braun, B., eds, 2001. *Social nature: theory, practice and politics*. Oxford: Blackwell.

Cosgrove, D., 1998. *Social formation and symbolic landscape*, 2nd edn. Madison: University of Wisconsin Press.

County of Fresno, 2014. *2014 Fresno county annual crop and livestock report*. Fresno, CA: County of Fresno.

Crouch, D., 2006. Tourism, consumption and rurality. In: P. Cloke, T. Marsden and P.H. Mooney, eds, *Handbook of rural studies*. London: Sage, pp. 355–364.

CSIRO, 2009. *Advice on defining climate scenarios for use in the Murray-Darling Basin Authority Basin plan modelling. MDBA technical report series: Basin Plan: BP01*. Canberra, ACT: Murray-Darling Basin Authority.

Department of Agriculture, Fisheries and Forestry, 2008. *An assessment of the impact of climate change on the nature and frequency of exceptional climatic events: drought exceptional circumstances*. Government of Australia. Online. Available at http://apo.org.au/node/6339 (Accessed 23 May 2015).

Department of the Environment, n.d. *Australian natural resources atlas: irrigation*. Available at: http://npsi.gov.au/products/pf010901 (Accessed 28 March 2013).

Department of Sustainability, Environment, Water Populations and Communities, 2011. *State of the environment*. Available at: www.environment.gov.au/soe/2011/report/inland-water/3-1-recent-climate.html (Accessed 23 July 2013).

Domosh, M., 1996. *Invented cities: the creation of landscape in nineteenth-century New York and Boston*. New Haven, CT: Yale University Press.

Edensor, T., 2006. Performing rurality. In: P. Cloke, T. Marsden and P. H. Mooney, eds, *Handbook of rural studies*. London: Sage, pp. 484–495.

Feldman, D.L., 2012. *Water*. Cambridge: Polity Press.

Franks, F., 2000. *Water: a matrix of life*. Cambridge: Royal Society of Chemistry.

Fresno Irrigation District, 2015. *History of the district*. Online. Available at: www.fresnoirrigation.com (Accessed 15 September 2015).

Goodwin, M., 2006. Regulating rurality? Rural studies and the regulation approach. In: P. Cloke, T. Marsden and P. H. Mooney, eds, *Handbook of rural studies*. London: Sage, pp. 304–316.

Gorman-Murray, A., Pini, B. and Bryant, L., eds, 2013. *Sexuality, rurality, and geography*. Lanham, MD: Lexington Books.

Grewal, I. and Kaplan, C., 2001. Global identities: theorizing transnational studies of sexuality. *GLQ: A Journal of Lesbian and Gay Studies*, 7(4), pp. 663–679.

Hanak, E., Lund, J., Dina, A., Gray, B., Howitt, R., Mount, J., Moyle, P. and Thompson, B., 2011. *Managing California's water: from conflict to reconciliation*. San Francisco: Public Policy Institute of California.

Haraway, D., 1988. Situated knowledges: the science question in feminism and the privilege of partial perspective. *Feminist studies*, 14(3), pp. 575–599.

Hinchliffe, R., 2003. People, plants and performance: on actor network theory and the material pleasures of the private garden. *Social and Cultural Geography*, 4, pp. 99–113.

Ingold, T., 1993. The temporality of the landscape. *World Archaeology*, 25(2), pp. 152–171.

Ingold, T., 2000. *The perception of the environment: essays on livelihood, dwelling and skill*. London: Routledge.
Lahiri-Dutt, K., 2014. Beyond the water–land binary in geography: water/lands of Bengal re-visioning hybridity. *ACME*, 13(3), pp. 505–529.
Laurie, N., 2005. Establishing development orthodoxy: negotiating masculinities in the water sector. *Development and Change*, 36(3), pp. 527–549.
Linton, J., 2010. *What is water? The history of a modern abstraction*. Vancouver: University of British Columbia Press.
Lyson, T.A., 2006. Global capital and the transformation of rural communities. In: P. Cloke, T. Marsden and P.H. Mooney, eds, *Handbook of rural studies*. London: Sage, pp. 292–303.
Macauley, D., 2006. The place of the elements and the elements of place. *Ethics, Place and Environment: A Journal of Philosophy and Geography*, 9(2), pp. 187–206.
Massey, D., 2006. Landscape as a provocation: reflections on moving mountains. *Journal of Material Culture*, 11(1/2), pp. 33–48.
Matless, D., 2003. Introduction: the properties of landscape. In: M. Domosh, S. Pile and N. Thrift, eds, *Handbook of cultural geography*. London: Sage, pp. 227–232.
Nelson, L., 2008. Racialized landscapes: whiteness and the struggle over farm-worker housing in Woodburn, Oregon. *Cultural Geographies*, 15, pp. 41–62.
Neuman, W.L., 2013. *Social research methods: Pearson new international edition: qualitative and quantitative approaches, 7e*. New York: Pearson Higher Education.
Nikolakis, W.D. and Grafton, R.Q., 2014. Fairness and justice in Indigenous water allocations: insights from northern Australia. *Water Policy*, 16, pp. 19–35.
Ong, A., 1999. *Flexible citizenship: the cultural logics of transnationality*. Durham, NC: Duke University Press.
Panelli, R., Hubbard, P., Coombes, B. and Suchet-Pearson, S., 2009. De-centring white ruralities: ethnic diversity, racialisation and Indigenous countrysides. *Journal of Rural Studies*, 25, pp. 355–364.
Patton, M.Q., 2002. Qualitative interviewing. *Qualitative Research and Evaluation Methods*, 3, pp. 344–347.
Pink, B., 2008. *Water and the Murray-Darling Basin: a statistical profile*. Canberra, ACT: Australian Bureau of Statistics.
Probyn, E., 2014. The cultural politics of fish and humans, a more-than-human habitus of consumption. *Cultural Politics*, 10(3), pp. 287–299.
Prosser, I.P., ed., 2011. *Water: science and solutions for Australia*. Victoria: CSIRO.
Prout, S. and Howitt, R., 2009. Frontier imaginings and subversive Indigenous spatialities. *Journal of Rural Studies*, 25(4), pp. 396-403.
Riverland Councils, 2012. *Submission to the Murray-Darling Basin Authority: a joint response by the Riverland Councils*. Available at: www.rdamr.org.au/fileadmin/user_upload/Murraylands/River_Murray/Riverland_Councils_Submission_Proposed_Basin_Plan_1_April (Accessed 23 July 2013).
Robinson, W.I., 2011. Globalization and the sociology of Immanuel Wallerstein: a critical appraisal. *International Sociology*, 26(6), pp. 723–745.
Rodríguez, S., 2006. *Acquia: water-sharing, sanctity and place*. New Mexico: School for Advanced Research Press.
Rose, G., 1993. *Feminism and geography*. Cambridge: Polity Press.
Sauer, C.O., 1925. The morphology of landscape. In: J. Leighly, ed., 1963. *Land and life*. Berkeley: University of California Press, pp. 55–103.

Steinberg, P.E., 1999. Navigating to multiple horizons: toward a geography of ocean-space. *The Professional Geographer*, 51(3), pp. 366–375.

Steinberg, P.E., 2001. *The social construction of the ocean*. Cambridge: Cambridge University Press.

Steinberg, P.E., 2014. Mediterranean metaphors: travel, translation, and oceanic imaginaries in the 'new Mediterraneans' of the Arctic Ocean, the Gulf of Mexico and the Caribbean. In: J. Anderson and K. Peters, eds, *Water worlds: human geographies of the ocean*. Aldershot: Ashgate, pp. 23–38.

Strang, V., 2004. *The meaning of water*. Oxford: Berg.

Sultana, F., 2009. Fluid lives: subjectives, gender and water in rural Bangladesh. *Gender, Place and Culture*, 16(4), pp. 427–444.

Tilley, C., 2004. *The materiality of stone: explorations in landscape phenomenology*. Oxford: Berg.

Tilley, C., 2006. Introduction: identity, place, landscape and heritage. *Journal of Material Culture*, 11(1/2), pp. 7–32.

United States Department of Agriculture, 2012. *Census of agriculture*. Washington, DC: Government Printing Office.

Vannini, P. and Taggart, J., 2014. The day we drove on the ocean (and lived to tell the tale about it): of deltas, ice roads, waterscapes and other meshworks. In: J. Anderson and K. Peters, eds, *Water worlds: human geographies of the ocean*. Aldershot: Ashgate, pp. 89–102.

Vara, V., 2015. Who's to blame for California's drought? *New Yorker*, 8 April. Online. Available at: www.newyorker.com/business/currency/whos-to-blame-for-californias-drought (Accessed 10 April 2015).

WeatherDB, 2015. Fresno, California average rainfall. Online. Available at: http://rainfall.weatherdb.com/1/37/Fresno-California (Accessed 15 September 2015).

Whatmore, S., 2006. Materialist returns: practicing cultural geography in and for a more-than-human world. *Cultural Geographies*, 13(4), pp. 600–609.

Wirf, L., Campbell, A. and Rea, N., 2008. Implications of gendered environmental knowledge in water allocation processes in central Australia. *Gender, Place and Culture*, 15(5), pp. 505–518.

Wylie, J., 2007. *Landscape*. Abingdon: Routledge.

Wynne, G., 2010. Foreword. In J. Linton, ed., *What is water? The history of a modern abstraction*. Vancouver: University of British Columbia Press, pp. ix–xvi.

Zwarteveen, M., 2008. Men, masculinities and water powers in irrigation. *Water Alternatives*, 1(1), pp. 111–130.

2 Contextualising water policy in irrigation communities

Introduction

The history of water policy development is often fraught with multiple complexities, relating to issues of ownership, governance and climate change. The difficulties associated with changing water policies which attempt to address these issues have been much deliberated in the international literature which examines water governance and policy entrepreneurship (e.g. Biswas and Tortajada, 2010; Crase, 2008; Crow, 2010; Head, 2010; Meijerink and Huitema, 2010). More recent literature in this area is especially concerned with the need for innovation which acknowledges the multiple, and often conflicting, social, economic and environmental priorities of water supply. In particular, Moore et al. (2014) provide a comprehensive overview of innovations in water policy, developing a typology which identifies not only the influence of technological changes, but also the requirement for *social* innovation. This acknowledgement of the social within water governance literature has been significant, recognising that shifts in water policy are not only legislative, but also lived within communities.

Focusing on the importance of the situated experience, this chapter provides the contextual basis upon which to explore the theoretical literature and concepts of water usage by examining historical shifts in water governance within Renmark and the Riverland region of South Australia, and Fresno and the wider Central Valley in California. Specifically, we examine the histories of policy development across the two sites, which share likenesses in water scarcity, settlement developments, and political complexities related to water usage. As Moore et al. (2014, p. 263) suggest:

> Understanding how policies change and the subsequent effect on practice is emerging as an important field of inquiry as governments, civil society, and industry look to address growing water quantity and quality concerns.

As sites which provide strategic international case studies on the social impacts of drought on agricultural communities, the Riverland and Central

California have endured repeated conditions of limited water supply and a necessity for the state to defend their water rights against other states whose users are supplied by the same river systems. Their historical development, environmental complexities, and policy trajectories also suggest that despite differences in geographic location and economic conditions, there is a shared experience of the problematic social impacts of shifting water policies, particularly during times of drought.

Policy development within Renmark and the Riverland, South Australia

Despite a well-rehearsed identity as the driest state on the driest continent in the world, South Australia's history of water management appears to be predicated upon several problematic assumptions, particularly in relation to irrigation. Beginning with colonial settlement, understandings of Northern European and later North American climates formed the basis for irrigation practices, promoting a continuous enlargement of water redirection. As a result, there have often been problematic interruptions to natural water flows, particularly in water-stressed regions (Cummins and Watson, 2012, p. 9). To understand the reasons behind these developments, we examine multiple sources, in particular Musgrave's (2008) comprehensive summary of irrigation history in Australia from early European settlement to the 1990s, in which he suggests there have been three significant phases in water policy, including early establishment, development, and reform. Since that time, Cummins and Watson (2012) have also suggested a fourth phase, which they term contraction.

The early establishment phase of irrigation appears to have begun immediately upon colonisation in 1788, forming an important aspect of the widespread nation building practices that were to follow during a time of seminal legislation. However, absent in this, and many other historical perspectives, is any detailed account of Indigenous activity in relation to hydrology prior to European settlement. More recent literature has begun to redress that gap, however, through comprehensive discussions on historical and contemporary Indigenous water knowledges and rights (Burdon et al., 2015).

According to Musgrave (2008), originally British settlers mistakenly expected a Northern Hemisphere system of hydrology which suits a system of water rights based on land's close proximity to water flows. Instead, though plentiful in some places, the absence of expected water flows meant that 'the appropriate institutions and works for the extraction and use of water were an inadequate and a troubled basis for the development of sound water policy over most of the nineteenth century' (Musgrave, 2008, p. 29). As a result, this early implementation of environmentally ineffectual strategies has since required the development of much more storage capacity and economic investment into water systems than might be expected from the same implementation within much of the Northern Hemisphere (Cummins and Watson, 2012).

From these beginnings, water continued to be a substantial focus of administrative and institutional attention during early settlement, encouraging greater immigration of European populations as the Australian agricultural industry grew in size and scope (O'Gorman et al., 2014). Irrigation projects were not always successful, however, and included several failed attempts at significant projects during the mid-nineteenth century in an effort to expand industry and counteract the effects of an Australia-wide depression (Alexander, 2005; Blackburn, 2004). As the issue of access to water became increasingly sensitive towards the latter half of the nineteenth century, numerous pieces of legislation were introduced across all states serviced by the Murray–Darling Basin, ensuring continued government involvement and intervention in matters of irrigation. Perhaps the most important of these was the Irrigation Act 1886 (Vic.), which gave each state complete control of its water, including individual citizens who might compromise the state's supplies (Mulligan and Pigram, 1989). Interesting for this book in particular, it seems that historically legislation in Australia has attempted to either replicate completely, or where not appropriate, ardently reject the water policy trajectories of California, in part based on the environmental challenges which followed the mid-nineteenth-century goldrushes in each place (Tyrrell, 1999). For example, in his creation of the Irrigation Act 1886 (Vic.), the future prime minister of Australia, Alfred Deakin, sought to avoid the Californian experience of numerous court actions to decide whose water rights were paramount. Instead, he opted to prioritise the rights of the state. Subsequently, in 1887, the Canadian born Chaffey brothers, both irrigation planners, were invited to Renmark and Mildura to establish irrigation colonies, based on their earlier success in establishing viable cities such as Etiwanda, Ontario and Upland in arid California (Cummins and Watson, 2012). Despite their subsequent financial failure in 1893, the importance of irrigation as the cornerstone of further development was established, allowing greater cultivation of the interior parts of Australia and Western Australia (Tyrrell, 1999). Through an Act of Parliament following their bankruptcy, the rights of the Chaffey brothers were then transferred to the Renmark Irrigation Trust, allowing settlers in the area to manage the local water resources, though state rights remained a priority. Eventually, the push towards centralised control of water would be cemented in the Water Act 1905 (Cth). This Act nationalised water rights, disestablishing most localised water trusts, and setting up centrally owned regulatory bodies who would control usage.

Once centralisation of water control was complete, most states associated with the Murray–Darling Basin began to focus more heavily on infrastructure, in particular storage facilities, creating a new era of development concentrated on a grandiose vision of continued nation building (Bellanta, 2008; Musgrave, 2008). Within South Australia in particular, politician David Gordon contended that irrigation would eventually allow Australia to become 'the economic centre of the Pacific' (Bellanta, 2008, p. 6). This confidence in irrigation was, in part, a wider acceptance of the importance of scientific ventures as an aspect of a 'rational society'. It was only during the 1960s, as financial concerns about government expansion into further irrigation projects became more prominent, that governments began to reduce their involvement, including subsidies. Concerns also began to surface regarding the environmental impacts of irrigation, which was originally developed at a time in which ecological principles were not prioritised (Blackburn, 2004). As Musgrave (2008, p. 39) argues, 'clearly the institutions created in the nineteenth century for development would no longer be appropriate. Fundamental reform would be necessary'.

During the era that followed, one which is still operational in many ways, analysis of the political discourse of water policy suggests there occurred a neo-liberal shift in water governance. Particularly in relation to the discourse of 'drought', economic policy became the primary marker of access to and use of water, eventually resulting in the introduction of water markets, allowing trading of water allocations between irrigators (Edwards et al., 2008). Prior to 1990, severe conditions of drought were understood as a form of natural disaster which might be roughly calculable but were not of the farmers' own making and were to be ameliorated through publicly funded assistance (Higgins, 2001). However, acceptance of this way of 'knowing' and managing the environment began to shift as part of the neo-liberal measures instituted by Australia's Labor government led by Bob Hawke (Vanclay, 2003). In the 1990s, governance became predicated on a move towards the deregulation of rural industries, requiring individuals to be entrepreneurs who could rationalise their farming practices and thereby effectively manage in times of drought (Gill, 2011). As such, climate change and more particularly, drought, continued to be understood as a threat to rural industries, but one whose risks could be controlled for through effective management by the individual (Tennberg, 2012) (see Chapter 5). As Higgins (2001, pp. 305–306) argues:

> Drought was brought into an advanced liberal domain of calculation through the linking of the natural environment – defined as a manageable risk – with farm management strategies … In other words, the existence or absence of drought was reconfigured within the capacities of farmers to conduct themselves in an entrepreneurial manner.

Moreover, with the introduction of water markets, the entrepreneurial push became more significant, at times motivating irrigators to apply for their maximum allocation, even if it was beyond their actual needs, in order to sell the resource on to another buyer. This may be understood as alternatively problematic and opportunistic, or as a regulatory mechanism which avoids difficult centralised administration and instead provides a useful way to allocate water to those who require it most (Adler, 2008, p. 16).

As part of this push towards efficiencies in water usage and concomitant concerns about environmental degradation during the late twentieth century, a cap was introduced following an audit of the Murray–Darling Basin. This cap limited the amount of water that could be diverted for New South Wales, Victoria and South Australia from 1 July 1997. As McKay (2008, p. 48) explains:

> Under the Cap arrangements, each state is required to monitor and report to the Murray–Darling Basin Commission (MDBC) on diversions, water entitlements announced, allocations, trading of water within, to, and from the state, and detail compliance with the target. The state must also report on measures undertaken, or proposed, to ensure that the water taken does not exceed the annual diversion target for every ensuing year.

This policy and several other government actions of significance that followed, in particular the Murray–Darling Basin Plan (MDBP), have highlighted the dual focus on the economy and the environment, under a neo-liberal framework. But perhaps the most significant development in Australian water policy has come from the establishment of the Council of Australian Governments (CoAG) reforms. These reforms included a national competition policy, in which many public bodies were sold to create funds which each state could access if they were to adopt what McKay (2008, p. 50) termed 'national water protocols'. Projects following these reforms were required to adhere to principles of environmental sustainability, whilst also involving greater local input from the community. Interestingly, this approach to reform appears to allow national bodies to retain control of the water resource whilst simultaneously devolving responsibility for its management to local areas (see Chapter 6). This prioritisation of economic sustainability, together with environmental considerations, has impacted considerably on the evolution of water policy. Stakeholders differentially concerned with economic versus environmental sustainability have created considerable tension during the development of legislation (Bark et al., 2014).

An attempt to address these inconsistencies was introduced through the National Water Initiative (NWI) in 2004. According to McKay (2008, p. 52), the NWI 'aims to achieve national compatibility in the markets, regulatory, and planning schemes to achieve sustainable management of surface and groundwater'. Thus, this initiative focused primarily on issues of efficiency, particularly through water pricing and environmental health. Following this was the introduction of the Water Act 2007 (Cth) and the Water Amendment Act 2008 (Cth), which established the Murray–Darling Basin Authority (MDBA). The MDBA was then in turn required to develop the Murray–Darling Basin Plan (MDBP), described as 'a strategic plan for the integrated and sustainable management of water resources in the Murray–Darling Basin' (Australian Government, 2015b). Specifically, the Plan aimed to restore the health of the Murray–Darling river system through restructured water allocations and water trading mechanisms that attempted to balance the needs of the environment with the needs of communities along the river (Gale et al., 2014). When conceptualised as part of the Water Act 2007 (Cth), for some, the envisaged MDBP represented optimistic possibilities for water reform (Quiggin et al., 2012). However, significant delays in the development of documentation and pre-release documents suggesting water allocation cuts of up to 30 per cent marked a period of anger and frustration within the irrigation community.

Introduced into law in 2012, the MDBP is expected to be fully implemented by 2019. Yet, for some, the plan was already seen as outdated even before its implementation, as its development occurred during a period of severe drought. Since this, many locations have experienced flooding, changing the basis upon which severe cuts were required, although this did not appear to alter the MDBP development. Most recently, there has been a call for a Royal Commission into what has been termed by one landholder as 'misinformation' about the MDBP. The proposed commission would allow the Senate Select Committee to examine how the plan had been communicated to those within the local communities affected, particularly in relation to economic and social outcomes (Corsetti, 2015). The Federal Government has identified their understanding of the importance of these outcomes, suggesting:

> The objectives of the Basin Plan include optimising social, economic and environmental outcomes arising from the use of Basin water resources in the national interest. The overall outcome sought ... is a healthy and working Murray–Darling Basin, which benefits those who live and work in the Basin, and people who visit and depend on its resources.
>
> (Australian Government, 2015a)

The government has also attempted to address concerns by detailing its framework for the evaluation of progress under the MDBP. Monitored by the MDBA, this evaluation tracks historic changes in community, assesses more recent effects of policy changes, and examines the ongoing experiences of individuals as the changes occur. Despite these indications of consultation, there remain concerns about the possible impacts of the MDBP, in particular declines in rural populations and fewer future opportunities for young people within agriculture. As Gale et al. (2014, p. 161) stated succinctly, 'Any coordinating governing body for the Murray–Darling Basin in the current political climate cannot address problems of the natural world without also considering social concerns'.

One body which consistently addresses policy shifts within the government's plan for the Murray–Darling Basin and represents a crucial point of examination of social relationships for this book is the Renmark Irrigation Trust. An irrigation service provider established in 1893 (Renmark Irrigation Trust, 2010), this community-owned organisation has been significant in the growth of the Renmark community, which itself is recognised as the first irrigation settlement in Australia. The Trust:

> recognises the need for healthy rivers to provide ecosystems that underpin the essential facets of good water quality, high biodiversity, healthy and sustainable food production, resilient land values, and to generate river linked tourism, that will support river communities such as Renmark.
> (Renmark Irrigation Trust, 2010, p. 1)

In their response to the MDBP, the RIT outlined the detrimental impacts that cuts to water allocations would have on the community. Like many individual irrigators and larger bodies representing irrigators, the RIT cited the substantial efforts made to ensure water savings through increased efficiencies. Further supporting these claims was a 'HotSpots assessment' done by the International Centre for Water from Charles Sturt University, which found the RIT delivery system was 97 per cent efficient (Renmark Irrigation Trust, 2010, p. 2). These efficiencies were achieved by the district's early adoption of, and investment in, effective water infrastructure. However, to install and service this infrastructure in turn requires high levels of horticultural production, suggesting that water cuts associated with the policy would have serious socio-economic impacts (Renmark Irrigation Trust, 2010, pp. 2–3). Though the MDBP was initially supported by many local irrigators who believed the centralisation of power might provide stronger representation for regional bodies, concerns for the future of the Riverland have been raised in relation to the proposed cuts within the changing water policy (see Chapters 5 and 6):

> The Basin Plan as described in the guide has a high probability of creating an unsustainable future for our communities as the lack of critical mass provided by irrigated agriculture will result in the knowledge and expertise in critical industries, loss of viable support services and significant concern that our major processors such as wineries, packers or beverage manufactures will leave!
> (Renmark Irrigation Trust, 2010, p. 4)

Moreover, like many districts in California, including the Central Valley, RIT argued that it is over-allocations of water in other states which impact upon the health of the water supply, rather than South Australian usage. This argument seems to reflect the complicated reality that multiple institutions with differing priorities are each contributing to policy developments, including local communities, state bodies, and the Commonwealth government. As Cummins and Watson argue (2012, p. 12):

> within the states and Commonwealth, there are multiple agencies involved in decision making, with different funding, disciplinary skills and agendas. The resultant blurred responsibility and confusion surrounding water policy is diminishing the dividend, from a substantial bureaucratic effort, not to mention imposing significant budgetary costs.

Responses to the ongoing development of the MDBP within Riverland communities and associated water governance have been mixed. Many irrigators have identified concerns about the uncertainty of water allocations (see Chapter 5) and communities remain frustrated by what they perceive as other states being unfairly prioritised before South Australia (see Chapter 6). There are also concerns that in attempting to address conflicts over water allocations between various stakeholders, the MDBP has simultaneously created a new set of challenges, particularly for South Australia. Suggestions that government funding be directed towards helping with infrastructure costs seem to ignore the significant efficiency measures already made by irrigators in the Riverland, where no new permits for water extraction have been granted since the 1960s (Government of South Australia, 2010). Moreover, there exist questions about the legitimacy of the MDBA, and its right to adjudicate between state and territory governments at the national level on behalf of the Commonwealth government (Gale et al., 2014).

Examining the impact of such changing water governance within the Murray–Darling Basin, Wallis et al. (2013) found that traditional governance methods are largely inadequate. Whilst useful in increasing regulation and ensuring adequate information provision, the MDBP still assumes there is a 'fixed' problem which can be addressed to the satisfaction of all members involved. Instead, following the now well-cited work of Rittel and Webber (1973), Wallis et al. (2013, p. 412) suggest the Murray–Darling Basin presents a 'wicked situation', which current planning reforms have not been able to successfully address. Instead, the reforms have contributed to a discrepancy between what key stakeholders, including irrigators, believe 'was' the current situation and 'what [it] ought to be'. In particular, there is concern about the centralisation of power in relation to water governance. Though state and federal governments advocate for an 'evidence-based' approach, many irrigators are concerned that this is primarily an attempt to legitimise political decisions through a scientific discourse, which may not reflect useful expertise for their own context. Thus, though emerging from drought conditions, Renmark, and more widely, Riverland areas of South Australia remain concerned about shifting water governance and resulting allocations, in terms of the environmental, economic and social challenges that lie ahead.

Policy development within Fresno and Central California, USA

When considering issues like drought, whether within the Australian or American context, it is important to recognise that however these issues are described, they are experienced within the community not only as natural events, but also as *social* events, influenced by human interests. In particular, this includes policies arising from the ideological and economic positions of those in power, and this is often where contestation and frustration arises most significantly. As Hanak et al. (2011, p. 7) argue:

> Each faction, while acknowledging the growing problems of decline, fears policy change and seeks only those changes that serve its own interests, thus collectively preventing anything but small changes in management despite growing prospects for catastrophe.

Further, as identified by the *Sacramento Bee* in its 28 May 2015 guide to California's water crisis:

> The problem isn't that no one foresaw the drought. The problem is that no one has been able to solve an underlying issue that is simultaneously less scary and also much harder than a dry spell: California's convoluted water system and intractable water politics. Designed piecemeal over the last century ... California's system for managing water doesn't just make it tough to deal with shortages – in some ways, it encourages inefficiencies and waste.
>
> (Plummer, 2015)

Like the earlier discussion of South Australia's Riverland, the history of California's water policy development within the Central Valley reflects the larger context of policy as ideologically connected to nation building. Many sources have rehearsed the complex nature of California's water policy history in more detail than is possible here (e.g. Attwater and Markle, 1987; Grantham and Viers, 2014; Hanak et al., 2011; Hundley, 2001). However, to understand the context of the Fresno and Central California case study site, it is important to highlight the most salient aspects of water policy development in California, and Central California specifically.

Historically, within California, access to water has been based on one of two sets of rights. The first is known as 'appropriative rights', given to the individual who first claimed the water for 'beneficial use', within an Act known as 'first-in-time, first-in-right'. This rough version of water policy was made essential by the Gold Rush of the 1850s when miners would collect and transport water far from its original source in order to assist with panning. Appropriative rights were officially recognised by the California legislature in 1851. However, 'riparian rights' were legislated in 1850, giving water access to those whose land holdings were physically nearest the waterway. Riparian rights did not require permits or licenses, as they did not apply to the owner, but instead the land upon which the water was naturally flowing past, and were not applicable to any water that was diverted for the purposes of storage or use in other locations. The hierarchy of these rights is complex. Riparian rights appear to be given priority, followed by appropriative rights, with those established prior to 1914 given priority within this category. As such, those who hold riparian rights and pre-1914 appropriative rights are considered the 'senior rights holders', and historically, it is understood both in policy and in discourse that these individuals have a 'right' to the water, and that it should be unrestricted. However, when a drought occurs, governing bodies which control water allocations can limit the rights of individuals, although these cuts are usually applied to junior rights holders first (Hanak et al., 2011; Hundley, 2001).

Also in question is the type of water being used by irrigators. Whilst surface water is more readily available in most cases, during times of drought or conflict as discussed above, groundwater may become more attractive. This is particularly true as historically, there have been far less limitations on groundwater, other than that extraction be of 'beneficial use'. Still, contemporary concerns have been raised regarding land subsidence and the decreasing groundwater table (Krieger, 2014). As Krieger (2014) explains: 'Overpumping not only lowers the water table and collapses land at the surface, but it also lowers water quality and requires more power to pump. River flows are lower, and shallow wells are exhausted.'

Returning to the issue of riparian and appropriation rights, these rights were developed during what has often been termed the first era of water policy in California (although like so many accounts, this tends to ignore the Indigenous histories that predate colonial settlement). In their account of historical developments in water policy, Hanak et al. (2011) identify the diversity of terrain and climate in the Californian landscape which can fluctuate between extremes of drought and flooding, resulting in ranges of 25–200 per cent of the average rainfall. In part, it is this diversity which has given rise to such multiplicity of both non-human and human life, including a complex linguistic landscape of more than eighty languages, spoken by more than 300,000 individuals during the eighteenth century (Anderson, 2005; Lightfoot and Parrish, 2009).

However, with the establishment of colonial control from 1769 onwards through the settlement of missions and pueblos by the Spanish and Mexicans, private and individual water rights became paramount. In particular, during the second half of the private holdings era (circa 1850–1870), water management was largely controlled by small groups without systematic organisation. Then, with the considerable population influx of the Gold Rush from 1848 onwards came the first industrialisation of water, eventually ushering in a new era of competition for the resource, and requiring new rules of allocation. Perhaps most interesting here are the ideological underpinnings of this initial era of water organisation and policy development in California, which suggests that the Gold Rush emphasised the importance of individualism. According to Hundley (2001, p. 67):

> Although Hispanic tradition and the long experience with aridity had produced a society stressing the preeminence of community rights and recognizing in government sweeping authority in allocating resources, the newcomers came from a tradition that valued individual rights and minimal government interference.

With the Gold Rush also came greater debris in the water ways due to sluicing, resulting in less capacity to carry water and combat flooding (Hundley, 2001). As a response, local reclamation districts were established, allowing landowners to come together to fund projects to help with flood control. However, because the levees created were stronger for some than others, many times the water simply travelled further down the system, flooding neighbours. As Hanak et al. (2011, p. 25) identified, 'In times of major floods, each district essentially relied on adjacent districts having levees weaker than their own.' As might be expected, by the late nineteenth century, this private rights approach to water development had become ineffectual, giving rise to a new era of local management.

During the second era of water policy development in California, public control was established through numerous local and state agencies, relying more heavily on groundwater as newer forms of technology allowed deeper drilling. The centrality of water at this time can be understood in part through several significant court cases and acts of legislation including the 1886 *Lux v. Haggin* (Cal.) which found that riparian rights surpassed those of the appropriation rights holders further upstream. Also important was the Wright Act of 1887 (Cal.), which created local irrigation districts, giving them eminent domain in order to curb the rights of private individuals, and ensure irrigation infrastructure would service the 'public good'. Later, in the 1903 case of *Katz v. Walkinshaw* (Cal.), a precedent was set that landowners would no longer have total rights to groundwater, limiting their access to a 'safe yield' to ensure the water table was not lowered to hazardous levels.

34 *Water policy in irrigation communities*

Interestingly, like many other regions, much of the water governance established by the legacy of private ownership and the resulting cases and legislation which followed is still in effect in the Central Valley region (Association of California Water Agencies, 2005).

Following the 1903 *Katz v. Walkinshaw* (Cal.) case came what is understood as the third era of public control which dominated the twentieth century, developing state-wide water projects and infrastructure. The influence of the concept of 'public good' during this time was such that in 1928, the Californian Constitution was changed so that all water law was based on 'reasonable and beneficial use', though the decision-making mechanisms were not clear. Various projects were initiated to deliver water to sites affected by drought and/or lack of water access annually. Of particular interest is the Central Valley Project, which allowed the Central Valley to flourish by storing water obtained in the northern part of the state in purpose built reservoirs and then transporting that water to locations in need. In what came to be known as the hydraulic era (Hundley, 2001), many large scale projects were established by state and federal bodies. For the Fresno Irrigation District in particular, the 1954 Pine Flat Dam project marked a substantial improvement in water supply stability, ensuring better flood control, storage and regulation of irrigation water. Fresno was also able to purchase water from the Friant Division of the Central Valley Project to further ensure adequate water supplies for irrigators (County of Fresno, 2015).

Though contention over access to water is a marked aspect of California's history, it is during the latter half of the twentieth century that the era of most significant conflict began. Termed the 'water wars', it was at this time that the type of water rights, the hierarchy of these rights, control of the resource and environmental concerns began to converge and challenge existing water policy. The impact of the large-scale projects also caused contention based on the wide disparity of water costs. Whereas coastal Southern Californian farmers were forced to pay up to $800 (per acre-foot) for their water because of associated transportation and infrastructure costs of the State Water Project, farmers further north paid only $8–40 (per acre-foot) due to their access to a larger number of local projects (Hanak et al., 2011, p. 93). Perhaps most problematic was the decentralised nature of the mechanisms of control and interest:

> Although state and federal agencies [have built] and operate[d] some of the largest water projects in California, the state's water management system is highly decentralized, involving many hundreds of local and regional agencies responsible for water supply, wastewater treatment, drainage managements, flood control, and land use decisions. This decentralization across scales and functions of government has created

many responsive but narrowly focused stakeholders who drive most water policy today.

(Hanak et al., 2011, p. 7)

Because of this complicated history, in Central California, many irrigators have attempted to 'pump at will', accessing groundwater without needing governmental approvals. However, with increasing concerns about environmental sustainability and the duration of the severe drought, it is recognised that surface and ground water cannot adequately address the needs of an increasing population, changing climate conditions, and the introduction of what have been more water intensive crops. Core to these issues is the fact that it is no longer possible to find new ways of accessing 'cheap' water, and the competition for what does exist is intense. This is particularly problematic given that the quality of the water available is often questionable. Thus, a more comprehensive strategy for water allocation and access is required. As Grantham and Viers (2014, p. 1) suggest:

> For 100 years, California's State Water Resources Control Board and its predecessors have been responsible for allocating available water supplies to beneficial uses, but inaccurate and incomplete accounting of water rights has made the state ill-equipped to satisfy growing societal demands for water supply reliability and healthy ecosystems.

By 2005, it had been more than 30 years since any large-scale improvements in Central California's water supply system. The Association of California Water Agencies (ACWA), formed in 1910 and responsible for 90 per cent of water supply delivery across California, identified the need for a water strategy that recognised the complexity of domestic and industrial demands. Its aim was to create 'a policy-oriented document that would encourage leaders at the state and federal level to re-engage in water issues and also provide a roadmap for investing in our water future' (Association of California Water Agencies, 2005, Foreword). Though increasingly a priority of the state, effective management of water security cannot be adequately addressed through the introduction of increased market mechanisms. Instead, the ACWA argues, a complex mix of community, infrastructure, governments, and industry is required to combat this problem (Association of California Water Agencies, 2005, p. 1).

An important issue raised by the ACWA is the recognition of the shifting input and control mechanisms of government bodies, both at the state and federal level (Association of California Water Agencies, 2005). As recognised in the historical overview discussed above, at one time governments led the way in infrastructure development. More recently, however, there has been a shift to greater local and regional efforts, perhaps echoing the neo-liberal approach discussed earlier, in order to create perceptual mechanisms of risk dispersal (see Chapter 5). The efforts of local organisations have been effective as a starting point, creating 4 million acre-feet of water storage through investments in water management. Yet, given the complexities of infrastructure and legislation, and the financial constraints of scale, it is unlikely that everything may be accomplished effectively at the local level. According to ACWA (2005), though local agencies are committed to working together to create the best outcomes for water supply, it is essential that the infrastructure used to deliver this supply is maintained at the state and federal level. Though this argument seems to oversimplify the complexities of water governance at the local level, it does reflect a wider body of literature which seeks to address ongoing tensions between local bodies and government authorities regarding responsibility, cost management, and expertise in water policy development (e.g. Biswas and Tortajada, 2010; Head, 2010; Olmstead, 2014; Sheikh et al., 2014).

More recently, the requirement for government intervention in conjunction with local action was recognised, following the severe drought that began in 2011. This was particularly important as California's Department of Water Resources is only able to *estimate* the volume of water supply used for different sectors in the absence of any true mechanisms of measurement, instead relying on self-reporting in most cases (Hanak et al., 2011, p. 86). In 2012, Governor Jerry Brown proposed the construction of a $23 billion series of tunnels to divert water to other parts of the state, in order to ensure a stable water supply for those communities. As the drought continued into 2014, Governor Brown declared a state of emergency and the public recognised the severity of the situation, voting to approve a $7.5 billion water bond. Similarly, lawmakers approved a $687 million drought relief package to assist farmworkers impacted by the drought (The *Bee* Editorial Board, 2015). But perhaps most significant was Governor Brown's introduction of legislation that required local agencies to manage groundwater resources (the Sustainable Groundwater Management Act – SGMA) with state intervention when necessary (see Chapter 6).

Fresno County was impacted by this change to legislation, situated over five groundwater sub-basins including Kings, Madera, Delta-Madera, Westside, and Pleasant Valley. All but Pleasant Valley are high-priority groundwater basins, meaning they are subject to a condition of critical overdraft and thus, a Groundwater Sustainability Plan (GSP) will need to be developed (County of Fresno, 2015). To achieve sustainable management, three steps are required. First, local agencies have to form Groundwater Sustainability Agencies by 2017; second, they will have to adopt the GSP in 5–7 years, depending upon the critical nature of the overdraft (much of Central California will be required to complete theirs by 2020); and finally, local agencies will have until 2040 to ensure the plans for sustainability are implemented (County of Fresno, 2015). Already, more recent agricultural adaptations to water scarcity have been significant, with overall water usage decreasing 13 per cent between 1960 and 2005, whilst per acre crop yields have improved by approximately 1.4 per cent per year (Hanak et al., 2011, pp. 88–89). However, as the severity of the drought continues, attention paid to irrigators and their water usage has increased. Thus, the continuing developments in water governance, associated legislation and irrigator responses will be crucial for the Central Valley area, and more widely the state of California. According to Hanak et al. (2011, p. 8), the status quo cannot continue, due to the severity of issues with:

> increasingly obsolete design of its water management systems, reductions in federal and state funding, changing climate, the challenge of incorporating environmental protection and sustainable management of the state's aquatic ecosystems, and lack of consensus on the options for future reform ... [which] have led California water management to a dysfunctional impasse.

The problematic outcomes resulting from these factors include a deterioration of ecosystems across the state, particularly in the Sacramento–San Joaquin Delta, which impacts significantly upon Central California. Also important will be the resulting issues with groundwater usage, fewer crops, the degradation of soil quality, environmental damage to fauna and flora, chemical poisoning of water supplies, and poorer water quality for rural users. Such challenges are substantial for Central California, made more complex by the multiple stakeholders whose interests inform the continuing shifts in water legislation and governance, both now and into the future (see Chapter 5).

Conclusion

This chapter has sought to overview the geographical and historical context of water policy development in the two distinct yet related sites: Fresno, in the Central Valley of California and Renmark, in the Riverland of South Australia. In providing an overview of their respective agricultural histories, water usage and particular irrigation practices, often the discussion has carried a dual focus on national developments in both the United States and Australia. This broader discussion is necessary as the centralisation of control over access to and use of water is a marked aspect of the water policy impacting on both communities.

Like any series of case studies, the sites examined here show distinct differences, particularly in their geographic locations and economies of scale. Yet these differences are minimal compared to the similarities of their environmental niche, their histories of drought and water legislation, and what may be the social and cultural impacts of these. As discussed in the introduction, water is not only a natural resource measured by gigalitres, but also part of a socio-natural system situated within a community context whose material reality is influenced by the 'social goals' of water policy development (Syme and Nancarrow, 2008). Economic, and more recently, environmental priorities, and the myriad ways these are often at odds, have impacted significantly on the evolution of water policy, underpinning many recent shifts in reform both in California and Australia. However, despite the material realities that are affected by these policies, the basis of water governance continues to be ideological in nature, resulting from political priorities, which themselves differ at the local, state and federal level. These complexities, their material realities and social impacts are examined in the remainder of the book.

References

Adler, J.H., 2008. Warming up to water markets. *Regulation*, Winter issue, pp. 14–17.

Alexander, A., 2005. *The companion to Tasmanian history*. Online. Centre for Tasmanian Historical Studies, University of Tasmania. Available at www.utas.edu.au/library/companion_to_tasmanian_history/index.htm (accessed 24 September 2015).

Anderson, M.K., 2005. *Tending the wild: North American knowledge and the management of California's natural resources*. Berkeley: University of California Press.

Association of California Water Agencies, 2005. *No time to waste: a blueprint for California water*. Sacramento: Association of California Water Agencies.

Attwater, W.R. and Markle, J., 1987. Overview of California water rights and water quality law. *Pacific Law Journal*, 19, pp. 957–1030.

Australian Government, 2015a. *Understanding the effects of water reform on basin communities and industries*. Available at: www.mdba.gov.au/socio-economic-profile-Murray-Darling-basin (Accessed 21 December 2015).

Australian Government, 2015b. *Water legislation*. Available at: https://www.environment.gov.au/topics/water/australian-government-water-leadership/water-legislation#water-act (Accessed 23 October 2015).

Bark, R., Kirby, M., Connor, J. and Crossman, N., 2014. Water allocation reform to meet environmental uses while sustaining irrigation: a case study of the Murray–Darling Basin Australia. *Water Policy*, 16, pp. 739–754.

Bellanta, M., 2008. Engineering the kingdom of God: irrigation, science and the social Christian millenium, 1880–1914. *Journal of Religious History*, 32(1), pp. 1–15.

Biswas, A.K. and Tortajada, C., 2010. Future water governance: problems and perspectives. *International Journal of Water Resources Development*, 26(2), pp. 129–139.

Blackburn, G., 2004. *Pioneering irrigation in Australia to 1920*. Victoria: Australian Scholarly Publishing.

Burdon, P. , Drew, G., Stubbs, M., Webster, A. and Barber, M., 2015. Decolonising indigenous water 'rights' in Australia: flow, difference and the limits of the law. *Settler Colonial Studies*, 5(4), pp. 334–349.

Corsetti, S., 2015. *Murray–Darling Basin plan: royal commission needed over 'misinformation', senators told*. Online. Available at: www.abc.net.au/news/2015-11-05/call-for-royal-commission-Murray-Darling-basin-misinformation/6916756 (Accessed 7 November 2015).

County of Fresno, 2015. Sustainable Groundwater Management Act. Online. Available at: www.co.fresno.ca.us/DepartmentPage.aspx?id=63723 (Accessed 16 September 2015).

Crase, L., 2008. *Water policy in Australia: the impact of change and uncertainty*. Washington, DC: RFF Press.

Crow, D.A., 2010. Policy entrepreneurs, issue experts and water rights: policy change in Colorado. *Review of Policy Research*, 4(1), pp. 27–41.

Cummins, T. and Watson, A., 2012. A hundred-year policy experiment: the Murray–Darling Basin in Australia. In: J. Quiggin, T. Mallawaarachchi and S. Chambers, eds, *Water policy reform: lessons in sustainability from the Murray–Darling Basin*. Cheltenham: Edward Elgar, pp. 9–36.

Edwards, J., Cheers, B. and Bjornlund, H., 2008. Social, economic and community impacts of water markets in Australia's Murray Darling Basin region. *The International Journal of Interdisciplinary Social Sciences*, 2(6), pp. 1–10.

Gale, M., Edwards, M., Wilson, L. and Greig, A., 2014. The boomerang effect: a case study of the Murray–Darling Basin Plan. *Australian Journal of Public Administration*, 73(2), pp. 153–163.

Gill, F., 2011. Responsible agents: responsibility and the changing relationship between farmers and the state. *Rural Society*, 20(2), pp. 128–141.

Government of South Australia, 2010. *Securing the future: a long-term plan for the Coorong, Lower Lakes and Murray Mouth*. South Australia: Government of South Australia.

Grantham, T.E. and Viers, J.H., 2014. 100 years of California's water rights system: patterns, trends and uncertainty. *Environmental Research Letters*, 9, pp. 1–10.

Hanak, E., Lund, J., Dina, A., Gray, B., Howitt, R., Mount, J., Moyle, P. and Thompson, B., 2011. *Managing California's water: from conflict to reconciliation*. San Francisco: Public Policy Institute of California.

Head, B.W., 2010. Water policy – evidence, learning and the governance of uncertainty. *Policy and Society*, 29(2), pp. 171–180.

Higgins, V., 2001. Calculating climate: advanced liberalism and the governing of risk in Australian drought policy. *Journal of Sociology*, 37(3), pp. 299–316.

Hundley Jr, N., 2001. *The great thirst. Californians and water: a history*. Berkeley: University of California Press.

Krieger, L.M., 2014. *California drought: San Joaquin Valley sinking as farmers race to tap acquifer*. Online. Available at: www.mercurynews.com/drought/ci_25447586/california-drought-san-joaquin-valley-sinking-farmers-race (Accessed 2 April 2015).

Lightfoot, K.G. and Parrish, O., 2009. *California Indians and their environment*. Berkeley: University of California Press.

McKay, J., 2008. The legal frameworks of Australian water. In: L. Crase, ed., *Water policy in Australia: the impact of change and uncertainty*. Washington, DC: RFF Press, pp. 44–60.

Meijerink, S. and Huitema, D., 2010. Policy entrepreneurs and change strategies: lessons from sixteen case studies of water transitions around the globe. *Ecology and Society*, 15(2), pp. 21–39.

Moore, M.L., van der Porten, S., Plummer, R., Brandes, O. and Baird, J., 2014. Water policy reform and innovation: a systematic review. *Environmental Science and Policy*, 38, pp. 263–271.

Mulligan, H.K. and Pigram, J.J., 1989. *Water administration in Australia: agenda for change*. Armidale, NSW: University of New England.

Musgrave, W., 2008. Historical development of water resources in Australia: irrigation policy in the Murray–Darling Basin. In: L. Crase, ed., *Water policy in Australia: the impact of change and uncertainty*. Washington, DC: RFF Press, pp. 28–43.

O'Gorman, E., Beattie, J. and Henry, M., 2014. 'Soothsaying' or 'science?' In: H. C. Russell, *Meterology, and environmental knowledge in rivers in colonial Australia: climate, science and colonization*. New York: Palgrave Macmillan, pp. 177–193.

Olmstead, S.M., 2014. Climate change adaptation and water resource management: a review of the literature. *Energy Economics*, 43, pp. 500–509.

Plummer, B., 2015. *A guide to California's water crisis – and why it's so hard to fix*. Online. Available at: www.vox.com/2015/4/10/8379221/california-drought-water-crisis (Accessed 2 April 2015).

Quiggin, J., Mallawaarachchi, T. and Chambers, S., eds, 2012. *Water policy reform: lessons in sustainability from the Murray–Darling Basin*. Cheltenham: Edward Elgar.

Renmark Irrigation Trust, 2010. *Re: The MDBA guide to the proposed basin plan*. Renmark, SA: Renmark Irrigation Trust.

Rittel, H. and Webber, M., 1973. Dilemmas in a general theory of planning. *Policy Sciences*, 4(2), pp. 155–169.

Sheikh, M.J., Redzuan, M.B., Samah, A.A. and Ahmad, N., 2014. Factors influencing farmers' participation in water management: a community development perspective. *ISOR Journal of Humanities and Social Sciences*, 19(11), pp. 59–63.

Syme, G.J. and Nancarrow, B.E., 2008. The social and cultural aspects of sustainable water use. In: L. Crase, ed., *Water policy in Australia: the impact of change and uncertainty*. Washington, DC: RFF Press, pp. 230–247.

Tennberg, M., 2012. Adaptation as a governance practice. In: M. Tennberg, ed., *Governing the uncertain: adaptation and climate in Russia and Finland*. London: Springer, pp. 17–35.

The *Bee* Editorial Board, 2015. Californians need a new mindset about water. *Fresno Bee*, 3 January.

Tyrrell, I., 1999. *True gardens of the gods: Californian–Australian environmental reform, 1860–1930*. Berkeley: University of California Press.

Vanclay, F., 2003. The impacts of deregulation and agricultural restructuring for rural Australia. *Australian Journal of Social Issues*, 38(1), pp. 81–94.

Wallis, P.J., Ison, R.L. and Samson, K., 2013. Identifying the conditions for social learning in water governance in regional Australia. *Land Use Policy*, 31, pp. 412–421.

3 Memory, place-making and water

Introduction

The centrality of water as a source of power and meaning within the narrative of human history can be traced through all societies, where water was and is understood as an essential resource underpinning existence. Interestingly, this enduring narrative suggests a stability and constancy that belies the continual ebbs and flows that characterise water's availability (Strang, 2004). Through the shifts which accompany both the developments of nature and of policy, our relationship with water similarly changes, understood over time as alternately a taken-for-granted resource, a lifeline, and a commodity, just to name a few. Water is also often used as a metaphor for time, forming the central subject matter for many songs and poems in which water marks the continual flowing of life (Strang, 2005; Tuan, 1968).

In this chapter, we aim to examine how the relationship between water and place-making shifts over time by tracing the narratives of meaning and emotion expressed by participants in relation to the two sites of study. Through the examination of these communities, we begin to understand the central importance of water as an aspect of place-making within both these particular sites of irrigation, and more broadly, any community where the availability or otherwise of this resource forms a historic and continuing structuring narrative. Thus, here, memory is centralised as the process by which water, and by extension, community, are given meaning over time. This chapter also theorises memory as a material process, simultaneously situated in and by the communities in which it is enacted (Hoelscher and Alderman, 2004). Thus, we examine how memory may be used as a form of place-making within irrigation communities, tracing the historical developments of knowledges, emotions and meanings around water, including changes in its purpose and availability. In this way, the chapter unpacks how narratives of water are contested, reconstituted and shift significantly to inform meanings of place and community over time, particularly during times of drought.

The way we were? Understanding collective memory and place-making

Though originally conceptualised by Halbwachs (1992) in his seminal work first published in 1925, more recently collective memory has been gaining greater traction both within and outside the academic domain as questions of inclusion, need and power highlight the selective and constructed nature of many histories (Weedon and Jordan, 2012, p. 143). Understanding the constructed nature of this memory is important as the narratives being recalled and ways of 'knowing' an essential resource like water are often not concerned primarily with historical accuracy, but instead with the meanings they bestow upon both the teller and listener. As Elsner explains:

> What matters ... is not that it be correct ... but that it be convincing to the particular group of individuals ... for whom it serves as an explanation of the world they inhabit ... what matters about any particular version of history is that it be meaningful to the collective subjectivities and self-identities of the specific group which it addresses. In other words, we are not concerned with 'real facts' ... but rather with the consensus of assumptions and prejudices shared.
>
> (1994, p. 226)

In this way, collective memory operates to contribute to Anderson's (1991) seminal concept of imagined communities, which here are understood not only as particular geographic locations but also communities of industry, specifically irrigators. Within the Riverland of South Australia, irrigators are drawn together collectively through the Renmark Irrigation Trust (see Chapters 5 and 6) whilst in California, a sense of collectivity may instead emerge from an irrigator's geographical and historical position within the complex water regulation systems.

In these imagined communities (imagined because no one can ever know all members or their practices), the shared sense of multiple aspects of identity may be more pronounced due to the capacity to 'know' a greater number of subjects and their histories (Anderson, 1991). Collective memory is also borne out by the centrality of primary industries in which water creates significant socio-spatial relationships of place by acting as a repository for aspects of collective meaning.

As part of this, memory is understood to operate on both the individual and collective level. Yet these may be difficult to separate, as remembering and forgetting are both actions influenced by the social group to which one belongs, where events are discussed and understood through a shared cultural lens (Wilson, 2005, pp. 39–41). This is not to deny the agency of the individual, suggesting that their memories are controlled solely by the community in which they live. Instead, collective memory may be best understood as situational, where subjects *use* the past to make sense of the present by actively selecting which memories and ways of 'knowing' they will recall and which aspects they will emphasise. This makes sense, given the pluralised nature of meaning subjects can create from the memories of even single events (Young, 1990). Thus, individual and collective memory work in a dialogic process, in which residents participate within the local social system and are influenced by it, but also possess the agency to act upon that social system. If so, questioning what has *really* happened within a community, in relation to the availability and control of water for irrigators, seems less important than considering what people *think* has happened and why those particular events and meanings are what they've chosen to believe and remember collectively:

> What versions of the past have they constructed and what meanings have they articulated to those constructions? Why do they – and we – remember some things and not others? What goes into the social construction of a past? And ... how are social memories struggled over, how are they used, and what effects do they have in the present?
> (Porreca, 1994, as cited in Wilson, 2005, p. 40)

In this way, collective memory may be understood as an aspect of community building, but one which is underpinned by elements of 'power, voice, representation and identity' (Weedon and Jordan, 2012, p. 143), in which certain subjects within the collective may be heard more readily than others (see Chapter 4). As such, collective memory provides an important concept through which to understand how a community's relationship to place – and in particular here, to water – and its members changes over time in particular ways of 'knowing'. As Edward Said (2002, p. 245) explained, 'People now look to this refashioned memory, especially in its collective forms, to give themselves a coherent identity, a national narrative, a place in the world.'

Telling 'stories': unpacking the relationship between collective memory and place-making narratives

Building on the work of Halbwachs (1992), memory is not only a collective practice, but as Hoelscher and Alderman (2004) also note, a *social activity* which is situated. Understood as a practice between subjects, we begin to recognise the constructed nature of landscape by examining how subjects work collectively to create meaning at particular sites through an active repetition of shared history and meanings, rehearsed over time. In this way, we echo Berger and Mohr's (1967, p. 13) original call to consider the social construction of landscapes:

Landscapes can be deceptive. Sometimes a landscape seems to be less a setting for the life of its inhabitants than a curtain behind which their struggles, achievements and accidents take place. For those who are behind the curtain, landmarks are no longer only geographic, but also biographical and personal.

According to the seminal work of French historian Pierre Nora (1989), 'sites of memory' (*les lieux de mémoire*) explains the way in which memory is understood to operate not only in material sites, such as churches, battlefields, and other locations within which the past may be enacted, but also in non-material sites, such as rituals, festivals, and more informally, conversation. It is within both these perceptual and material spaces of commonplace practice that Hoelscher and Alderman (2004, p. 350) suggest 'memory and place are woven into the fabric of everyday life'.

Thus, the rehearsal of meanings, or 'the storytelling of place' which rely on collective memory for construction are understood as simultaneously physically situated, but also performative, in which the repeated statement of meanings shared both formally and informally represent a cultural practice that works continuously to inscribe particular understandings on the landscape (Cresswell, 2004). In this way, place attachments may be formed, creating a sense of connection between an individual, their collective group and a landscape, based on both its material and non-material attributes. It is in this nexus between the material and the meanings made of these settings that we examine the narratives of irrigators in the Riverland and in Central California, in order to understand their shifting identifications of the centrality of water to the lived experience within these communities.

In particular, we seek to examine *how* place is given meaning. According to Tuan (1991), this is primarily a linguistic process, in which naming lays claim to place through street names and warm conversations between people contribute to building a particular atmosphere. Similarly, de Certeau's (1984) seminal study of 'walking the city' highlights the ways in which the body acts as a storytelling device, where space is enacted by our very presence and understandings within it. Many scholars (e.g. Arkaraprasertkul, 2012; Chronis, 2012; Cresswell, 2004; Derrien and Stokowski, 2014; Gutsche and Robert, 2014; Johnston, 1990) also highlight the importance of storytelling as the basis upon which place is constructed and understood because of its ability to create emotional connections. Alkon and Traugot's (2008) study of the situated relationship between policy and the social construction of place in two communities in California demonstrates how narratives were the means by which place was experienced and explained. Within these narratives, they identified two processes in the social construction of place: place comparison, in which residents highlighted both risks and opportunities in their community through comparisons with other communities, and place meta-narratives, in which residents utilised trope-based place narratives to discuss their own location.

Like Alkon and Traugot (2008), we recognise that although the construction of place is well rehearsed in a large body of literature examining place-making across the globe (e.g. Berger and Luckmann, 1991; Cresswell, 2004; Hoelscher and Alderman, 2004; Relph, 1976; Said, 2002; Tuan, 1977), our own contribution is made in emphasising those narrative processes by which place construction is made possible. Following the work of Derrien and Stokowski (2014), who studied the construction of sense of place over time through the narratives of Bosnian immigrants in Vermont, we examine *how* language is used to make meaning. We also examine how these patterns shift over time when the absence of water challenges narratives and the memories upon which they are constructed. As Derrien and Stokowski (2014, pp. 108–109) argue:

> Narrative research is particularly suitable for addressing the social construction of sense of place because it is grounded in theories that conceptualize discursive processes as on-going social actions ... Moreover, a fundamental characteristic of narrative – a plot that incites transformation over time – directs attention to social processes and cultural contexts over time and not simply to independent experiences or personal meanings.

We recognise, however, that these narratives are selective, in terms of what is remembered and what is forgotten, both on an individual and a collective basis. In Riverland and Central Californian irrigation communities, there exists a significant engagement with a colonial past, where only certain stories and versions of history are highlighted in order to animate the present (see Chapter 4). This is an important consideration for this research as a sense of inclusion is central to collective memory, as subjects identify (or otherwise) with the narratives which circulate within particular locations, explaining how a place and the subjects therein have developed over time (Weedon and Jordan, 2012). Within this, the power to influence both the content and the circulation of these narratives represents a possible point of contestation for those who are excluded and whose histories do not form part of the community narrative. We are thus mindful of these presences and absences within the narratives discussed below and examine the complexity of these multiplicities in more detail in Chapter 4.

Making 'sense' of place: tracing narrative development of place within irrigation communities

The narratives which formed the main focus of irrigators' attention in both the Riverland and Central California consistently referred to the multiple meanings of water, though their understandings of these appeared to differ greatly in relation to purpose. Such a concentration on water as a central aspect of the meanings irrigators attach to 'place' suggests then a need to understand how the narratives built over time reflect the collective memories of communities affected by drought. As the availability of water diminishes or appears uncertain, whether through natural drought or government policy, these memories and meanings may be disrupted, challenging how irrigators understand their communities and the aspects of collective identity that reside therein. In the following section, we unpack the themes raised within these two communities to highlight the shifts and slippages in their narratives about water and its presence/absence in their communities.

In the Riverland, the importance of water in sustaining communities over time was consistently raised by participants, many of whom identified the Murray River as the 'lifeblood' of their community and went further to suggest that without adequate water allocations (or with allocations offered only at an inflated cost), the community itself would become unsustainable.

> it's like your blood running through your body I suppose. It's part of your life, it's always there; it would be devastating not to see it there ... it brings on a lot of social events, brings a lot of people together ... it's our lifeline to the area, well to everybody really ... without water none of us would survive.

> it's the lifeblood of this part of Australia, as beautiful as it is and where there's water, there's always going to be life, but when you look into it, especially like us when you rely on water so much, it's probably more than that...we're pretty grateful about it, we have such a good 'backyard' to be honest ...

> a lifeline ... I can't say it's my hobby or interest, I just keep getting stuck at lifeline. Without the Murray, this community wouldn't be here.

> essentially, if the Murray River wasn't here, we wouldn't be here. And you can drive up the Murray River and walk two kilometres inland from the river and it's a barren desert. I mean, the only reason we're here is because of irrigation and river water ... without the Murray, there's nothing.

Though this kind of valuing of water is not unexpected within locations like the Riverland, which relies so significantly on irrigation, what is notable is the language used to describe the water's purpose, which appeared to go far beyond a utilitarian consideration of need. Instead, the language seemed to speak to an embeddedness in aspects of community identity which resonate at the individual level. This expression of place attachment, described as 'lifeblood', 'lifeline', 'always there', seems to reflect the ways in which places serve as 'emotional centres of meaning' (Derrien and Stokowski, 2014, p. 107), an enduring relationship which has been identified repeatedly by researchers across multiple domains within the social sciences (e.g. Alkon and Traugot, 2008; Arkaraprasertkul, 2012; Cresswell, 2004; Derrien and Stokowski, 2014; Gutsche and Robert, 2014; Kyle and Chick, 2007; Manzo, 2003; Milligan, 1998; Potter, 2010).

This importance of emotions as an aspect of place is centralised within the field of emotional geographies, which speaks into the ways in which the 'human world is constructed and lived through the emotions' (Anderson and Smith, 2001, p. 7). This recognition is challenged equally, however, by the difficulties in conceptualising emotions, as they resist simple taxonomies, instead slipping between the universal and the personal through distinctions of experience, moment, and impact (Ahmed, 2000; 2004). In her examination of the importance of the physical within the emotional, Probyn (2004) explains that emotions are not only socially manifested but also possess a material presence, marked upon and by the body of the subject. Like Ahmed, Probyn interrogates the complexity of emotions to understand the ways in which they move beyond the discursive to the material, both for the subject and for the places they inhabit. In this way, the relationships between individuals and 'their places' are captured within 'emotional landscapes', where the complexities of the spatial and temporal are enfolded, shaped, and embodied in particular contexts (Bryant, 2015). As Davidson and Milligan (2004, p. 524, emphasis in the original) explain:

> Without doubt, our emotions *matter*. They have tangible effects on our surroundings and can shape the very nature and experience of our being-in-the-world. Emotions can clearly alter the way the world is for us, affecting our sense of time as well as space. Our sense of who and what we are is continually (re)shaped by how we *feel*.

Here, the importance of emotion is embedded within participants' narratives of water, where irrigators work to situate the river as a treasured friend, intimate in its familiarity and necessity. The river is not simply a recreational site, but instead generative of a deeply felt expression of individual and community 'essence' which is marked by a reverence for the river's contributions to the continuation of a particularly situated shared existence. The metaphor of 'lifeblood' used by multiple participants marks the river as a physical presence whose existence mirrors and intertwines with their own, anthropomorphising the river as a means by which to articulate its value. The importance of the river's presence is also highlighted by the implicit narratives of fear that arise in considerations of alterations in its flows. The focus on the river's constancy ('it's always there'), and its possible loss is recognised as a source of not just sadness, but devastation by many, suggesting an urgency which underlies a deeply embedded fear of absence. These emotional 'riverscapes' support the work of Kearns and Collins (2012), whose study of the feelings evoked by coastal places under threat found a complicated mix of reverence, connection and anxiety. Though the study was situated in New Zealand specifically, these findings seem to reflect a shared experience of the centrality of place internationally (Creswell, 2004). As Van Patten and Williams (2008, p. 449) argue, 'people attach meaning and significance to specific places that often coincides with the formation of deep emotional attachments or bonds'.

The significance of these bonds is further underscored by a sense of fragility that appears in the Riverland narratives when referring to the future and their dependence on water as a resource. Interestingly, for many this fragility appeared only as a future consideration, removed from any associated cyclical understanding of water's past absence in the community, although one participant did highlight previous experiences with drought:

> I suppose we're fortunate that the locks held the water here, that we didn't have to see it in its worst state because my mum, I mean, they've got photos of when they walked across the river at Berri ... before the '56 floods, and you know, to see that now would be horrible.

In this way, the ebbs and flows of water are recognised as variable, but the conditions of drought are not normalised despite previous experiences. Instead, the absence of the river is understood as an aberration that would have dire consequences for the community. Over time however, as drought conditions became more pronounced, for some, there was a notable shift within their narratives, acknowledging the enormity of the river's presence in the community, but also a tangible sense of loss, as its flows ebbed and changed.

> In a longer term, and here I'm talking about many years ... there's been a real change in the way people think about water ... in the very early stages it was thought of an unlimited commodity and we've been through a journey of realising that's not the case and the community has made some change around that.

> I used it as a kid, right ... But my concern is that our children and other people who live in our town ... they're the ones that are going to be missing out ... the way it is at the moment, there's still some greatness in the river; that's why we're still here. It's a magnificent river, and so many people enjoy it.

This interruption to water flows marks a significant change in narrative, as the second participant in particular traces memories of past abundance and presence to a contemporary threat of absence and a resulting concern for a future loss of community. The threads of this narrative reflect a reshaping of ideas about community, based on the impacts of drought, as the individual's sense of place is rendered more vulnerable. The memories of the river's strong presence imply and inform a recalled sense of community, reflected in the language of 'concern' for community members and their experience in the present. In their study of drought conditions in New South Wales, Australia, Albrecht et al. (2007) provide a useful theorisation of this kind of distress, which they term 'solastalgia', or the emotional responses, often negative, to the effects of changes in the environment over time. Although difficult to rehearse in full here, there is a further large body of research on distress during times of drought (e.g. Bryant and Garnham, 2013; McManus et al., 2012; Ng et al., 2015; Sartore et al., 2008; Verrinder and Talbot, 2015; Wilson et al., 2015) which suggests that the absence of water within irrigation communities has significant impacts on the social, environmental, and political meanings subjects make of place over time.

As the drought in the Riverland extended, it is interesting to note that the impact on community appeared to be one in which many members experienced a greater level of support from one another, further fortifying their sense of place through a strengthening of community ties. Thus, as meanings of water became more fraught during drought, the disruptions to meanings of place were ameliorated somewhat by the shared sense of community (see Chapter 6). As one participant commented:

> so, good times and bad, you know – you all go through it together, and so, whether that be family situations, or whether it be economic situations, you all go through it together.

As such, it appears that in the Riverland, the narratives which explain how water is understood in the community over time, and how that in turn contributes to sense of place, are often emotional in nature, describing water, both its presence and absence, in terms which speak to a deeply embedded place attachment for most subjects.

In contrast, in Central California, meanings of water over time were often expressed in narratives of pragmatism, concentrating on water's purpose as a resource for growth rather than an emotionally embedded aspect of community. These understandings about what water *is* and what it should *do* conceptualise water as a commodity which is often contested at multiple levels and whose importance is primarily reflected in economic terms (see Chapter 5). Of course, the discourse of economics has always been prevalent in agricultural communities in both Australia and the United States, where complex equipment and increasingly sophisticated technologies require large operating budgets. However, the difference in concentration on narratives of water's meaning for a community to narratives of water's economic utility is marked, as the control of water becomes increasingly centralised (Strang, 2004, p. 36). Particularly within drought conditions under neo-liberal ideologies, water becomes conceptualised as a scarce resource whose value is significantly increased, and thus a product which may be allocated, traded, auctioned, bought and bought back (Bjornlund et al., 2010; Iftekhar et al., 2013; Loch et al., 2012; Zetland, 2013). According to Worster (1985, p. 52) in his examination of the implementation of what he termed 'The Capitalist State Mode' of production, this increasing shift towards a focus on water as an economic object rather than a natural one has significant outcomes for those who would use it:

> The most fundamental characteristic of the latest irrigation mode is its behaviour toward nature and the underlying attitude on which it is based. Water in the capitalist state has no intrinsic value, no integrity that must be respected. Water is no longer valued as a divinely appointed means for survival, for producing and reproducing human life, as it was in local subsistence communities. Nor is water an awe-inspiring ally as it was in the agrarian states. It has now become a commodity that is bought and sold.
>
> (Worster, 1985, p. 52)

In this way, the intimacy of the relationship between the irrigator and water may become increasingly alienated over time, as simultaneously, the distance between those who control the water and those who use it intensifies. In discussions with irrigators from Fresno in particular, each individual was keen to rehearse the history of water legislation development (see Chapters 2 and 6). Initially, each rehearsal varied somewhat, with some focusing on the history of particular individuals and others on the types of legislation developed over time. However, when focused on the modern era of irrigation all narratives appeared to shift, becoming primarily concerned with economics and water availability, aligned with the financial viability of their farms. Thus, emotional notions of water were eschewed for more pragmatic meanings. As one participant identified when asked about the impact of drought:

> Well, you make a decision on the dollars of profit per acre food and water. That's how you do it – plain and simple. And it might mean that you grow broccoli in the winter time and use 12 inches of water instead of 4 feet. I have broccoli over here right now. We're going to probably use a foot and a quarter of water and we're going to gross $4,000 dollars but

hopefully make $1,500 – well, that acre foot brought me $1,500. That might be better – because almonds to do the same – where they use 4 acre feet of water – they would have to bring me $6,000. So that's the decision.

In this way, a choice is made to invoke narratives of pragmatic decision making. In response to a request to explain his experience as an irrigator during the absence of water, the participant avoids any comment on changes in the place itself or its meaning for the individual beyond economic terms. Even in participants' rehearsals of the ebbs and flows of water in the area over time in which they start to speak to the impact of disrupted water flows, the meaning of water remains an economic one:

we had the last drought from '87 to '92, was a pretty long one, they were talking about people were going to start leaving California because in the desert empire water's definitely the most valuable thing.

The effect of this economic focus, which allocates water's meaning as a financial one, and in so doing, positions it as a commodity, is substantial. Sense of place within rural communities is defined not only by the personal histories of residents, the rituals and events which take place there and the features of the material site itself, but also by the local industries which contribute to residents' livelihoods (Cloke et al., 2006). The position of agriculture within irrigation communities is often a source of pride, with many heralding their particular produce or position within the industry on signs welcoming visitors to town (e.g. Fresno, the 'raisin capital of the world'; Gilroy, the 'garlic capital of the world', Central California, 'the largest supplier of canned tomatoes', etc.). If water's position within the community is equated to that of other 'commodities', irrigators may then reasonably consider which 'commodity' will deliver the greatest economic return, resulting in instances where agricultural livelihoods are based in part on trade which involves the production of no actual foodstuffs. As several participants identified:

The question is, how can they make the most money? By selling their water or by growing a crop? The water in many cases now, exceeds the value the crop produced ... These guys are not farmers first, they're businessmen first.

A lot of guys are going to say 'Hell, farming is risky, the water is more valuable than the crop.'

In examining how the collective memory of water influences place-making in Central California, it was also interesting to note the inferred relationship identified by some participants between the positioning of water as a commodity and a community under significant strain of fracture. In part, there seemed to be an absence of place attachment resulting from a disconnect between the individuals who own the land and the land itself. Several participants identified an increasing divide between those who own the farms and those who service them:

> It's unbelievable how many people come out here every day, but there is a whole movement of labour every day at certain times of the day when they're either going home or coming to work … the reality is people live where they are with their own type.

> you know this is poverty … Land owners don't live in these communities, they live in Fresno … Some people call them plantation owners.

In contrast, in those locations where subjects actually live in the communities in which they irrigate, there seemed to be a greater sense of place attachment for residents. Often, this was predicated on the notion that irrigators with smaller land parcels experience decreased instances of labour tensions because of their personal relationships with those who work the land. These complex social aspects of labour relations and the physical presence of the irrigators themselves thus represent an important contribution to understandings of community (Bonanno, 2015). In the absence of material experience of the land built over time through personal engagement, subjects may feel a sense of disconnection, resulting in irrigators who are not as significantly invested in contributing to 'place'. Moreover, in their absence, neither are their memories actively circulated within the community, such that both their parcel of land and their individual selves do not actively inform the situated collective memory of those sites.

It may be that this difference in meanings of water and thus emotional attachment to place between the Riverland and Central California results in part from the way in which water's presence is physically manifested within the community. Water supplies to many parts of Central California are made possible by infrastructure which transports the resource from bodies of water that aren't necessarily visible within the community, and are delivered via particular manmade structures that were always intended to deliver stability. In contrast, in the Riverland water flows right through the community as a large and winding river, whose ebbs and flows are always visible, acting as a material focal point upon which collective memories of the community are built.

'But what are we handing down?' Considerations of memory, meaning, and place-making in issues of succession

Whilst understandings about the meaning of water and its impact on place-making differ across locations, the centrality of water to the working practices of both the Riverland and Central California is evident. When water's presence is threatened by disruptions to flows, as experienced in times of drought, there may be a challenge to often static temporal notions of memory which assume a particular future based on what has come before (see Chapter 6). As suggested by several participants, drought and changing water allocations are not just a condition of water, but also a condition of the community. Through these responses, we begin to understand how the sense of place informed by the collective memory which evolved over multiple generations of irrigators is challenged, as the ways of understanding both water as a resource and agriculture as an industry, shift and change, particularly in relation to issues of succession (Gill, 2013).

The importance of succession was highlighted recently by the United Nations General Assembly, which declared 2014 the 'International Year of Family Farming'. Globally, farming remains primarily a family enterprise, though there is significant concern that this trend appears to be declining due to changing environmental concerns, neo-liberal policy developments and increasingly complex global trade conditions (Brandth and Overrein, 2013; van Vliet et al., 2015; Wheeler et al., 2012). Resulting changes in the transition patterns of farms represent a possible threat not only to the families involved but also their communities (Fischer and Burton, 2014). Exploring these relationships between time and place, Gill (2013) suggests succession represents a particularly important temporal act, as it requires that families understand not only their own histories, but also the historical and social positioning of their land within the context of the community in order to negotiate the most appropriate successor to continue the family legacy:

> The successful transition of property between generations within the family ensures continuity for both family on the farm and *the community in which the farm is located*.
>
> (Gill, 2013, p. 76, emphasis added)

This interplay between family and community considerations was evident in our discussions with irrigators, who each identified how long they and their families had been 'on the land' (see Chapter 6). As a practice, this spoke immediately to their presence as part of the collective memory of place through their identification of irrigation as a multi-generational project. It was here, in the resulting issue of succession and future generations, that we see the strongest similarities in responses from Riverland and Central Californian irrigators. As Wheeler et al. (2012, p. 266) suggest, 'Agriculture is an inherently uncertain enterprise'. However, any possible complacency that might arise from the ongoing nature of this uncertainty was belied by the emotion conveyed by irrigators in both the Riverland and Central California when discussing succession. Where there were concerns about the likelihood that the drought would break *before* individuals were forced to sell their land parcels, there was a tangible loss of place and community threatened by an end to succession within families.

> I think we're probably on the cusp. There's always been this 'we'll be alright, we'll be alright' you know? ... and I think generally, [irrigators] are a proud people, and so they won't complain a heck of a lot. But I can see where people are, as families, changing direction. They are encouraging their children to go and do something else because they really believe that there isn't a lot of future.

The centrality of the material site to the emotional landscapes experienced by individuals was evident in these and other narratives, reflecting unspoken spatial entanglements of a place unfinished, 'woven together out of ongoing stories' (Massey, 2005, p. 131). Yet, in many cases, the desire to remain, even to endure, so that the family's history within the community remained as part of the legacy of that place, was at odds with the realities faced by irrigators. Many spoke in particular of their children wanting to continue with the business but the equal impossibility of this due to the unpredictability of drought conditions and water allocations. Largely, respondents seemed concerned that they did not want to watch the next generation struggle as they had.

> Our elder son would like, well, all of the kids would like us to keep the block but we wouldn't put the stress that we go through ... they couldn't handle it ... it would just ruin their lives.

> I've got no succession plan in place ... I don't believe there's a great future in what we're doing long term. I think we're kidding ourselves ... we seem to be in a pressure cooker ... why would I try and push one of my sons into doing what I'm doing?

This absence of a succession plan reflects a complicated understanding of the relationship between past and future, where the situated memory of what has come before is challenged by complex notions of uncertainty, loss and grief. Even to acknowledge that the farm may not be transferred to the next generation carries with it notions of shame and failure (Bryant and Garnham, 2015).

> When you've lost the farm, you've lost everything.

Memory, place-making and water 55

Yet the challenge to succession is not always so tangible, nor so immediate. In many ways, it is the long-term pressures which slowly erode underlying practices of place, slightly altering everyday routines, family habits and community behaviours to compensate for changes over time. As one participant explained, possibilities of succession are not 'suddenly' given up. Instead, like the building of collective memory and place meanings, which inform these decisions, the process is incremental and unseen, eventually making particular paths impossible because of changes in water availability.

> I can't say that I've seen a lot of families just get up and walk off. What tends to happen is, first of all, families come together around a farming enterprise, so before the family would have worked as an extended family, a father and maybe a couple of sons. That doesn't happen anymore. The father will stay put; the sons will go off and do something else. So it sort of breaks families up ... it's not a 'here's something that has formed, and that has broken apart', it's something that just never forms. I can't tell you any kids that have gone to work in family farming enterprises; they just don't do that anymore.

Within this narrative is an implicit chronicling of loss, in which the traditions of a family and more widely, the community in which it is situated, are threatened and eventually, overwhelmed by the circumstances around them. Therein exists a sense of finality, in which the cyclical operations of irrigation are permanently undone, separating the assumed multi-generational presence of individuals from the land in which they reside. In this way, the issue of succession is recognised as part of the larger discussion about the ways in which water is understood in relation to community and time, where the foundations of past place-making are challenged by the erosion of future possibilities (see Chapter 6).

Conclusion

Concerns and contestation over water, its availability and its ultimate purpose, have been a recurrent narrative thread in many communities. Numerous scholars have given their attention to these historical tensions, highlighting the shifting conceptualisations of water resulting from early changes in farming technology to later developments of the industrial revolution, to ongoing moves towards privatisation and centralised control. As part of this continuing narrative, this chapter examined not how water has been *used*, but instead how it has been *understood* and brought into a particular kind of existence(s) through narrative, circulated within communities to create certain ways of 'knowing' this resource. Through the narratives of irrigators within the Riverland and Central California, we begin to understand how the shifts of water flows direct and reflect the centrality of water as an aspect of place-making and how that is enacted in particular communities. Studies on irrigation processes support recognition of these more social aspects of irrigation communities, including in particular Edwards et al.'s (2008) study of the impact of water markets on the Murray–Darling Basin region in Australia. Arguing that the prioritisation of economic considerations over social ones may have serious consequences for rural communities, they suggest, 'community members regard water and its tie to their locality as the foundation of their wealth and vibrancy' (Edwards et al., 2008, p. 966).

As this 'tie' is challenged, so too then are notions not only of 'place' but also of temporality, where memories of the past and their associated meanings inform place-making in the present. Based on the findings of this chapter, these meanings appear to move across and between concerns about production, livelihood and the centrality of water in eliciting emotions and a sense of belonging to place.

The recognition of emotion as central to the collective narratives of place-making represents an important contribution to the study of drought-affected places, explaining the ways in which these landscapes, or more specifically here, 'waterscapes', are imbued with a structure of feeling that is intensified during times of threat. Moving between appreciation, reverence, trust, anger and fear, irrigators in the Riverland and Central California narrate the physical presences and absences of water, mobilising the importance of the material to the human experience. The emotions are never static, conveying a complexity of attachment that explains how the communities in which we reside and work are not simply sites upon which to act, but instead form the repositories of collective memory that imbue place with meaning.

References

Ahmed, S., 2000. *Strange encounters: embodied others in post-coloniality*. London: Routledge.

Ahmed, S., 2004. *The cultural politics of emotion*. Edinburgh: Edinburgh University Press.

Albrecht, G, Sartore, G.M., Connor, L., Higginbotham, N., Freeman, S., Kelly, B., Stain, H., Tonna, A. and Pollard, G., 2007. Solastalgia: the distress caused by environmental change. *Australasian Psychiatry*, 15(1), pp. 95–98.

Alkon, A.H. and Traugot, M., 2008. Place matters, but how? Rural identity, environmental decision making, and the social construction of place. *City and Community*, 7(2), pp. 97–112.

Anderson, B., 1991. *Imagined communities*. London: Verso.

Anderson, K. and Smith, S.J., 2001. Editorial: emotional geographies. *Transactions of the Institute of British Geographers*, 26(1), pp. 7–10.

Arkaraprasertkul, N., 2012. Moral global storytelling: reflections on place and space in Shanghai's urban neighbourhoods. *Storytelling, Self, Society: An Interdisciplinary Journal of Storytelling Studies*, 8(3), pp. 167–179.

Berger, J. and Mohr, J., 1967. *A fortunate man*. New York: Pantheon.

Berger, P. and Luckmann, T., 1991. *The social construction of knowledge: a treatise in the sociology of knowledge*. Harmondsworth: Penguin.

Bjornlund, H., Wheeler, S. and Cheeseman, J., 2010. Irrigators, water trading, the environment and debt: buying water entitlements for the environment. In: D. Connell and R. Grafton, eds, *Basin futures: water reform in the Murray–Darling Basin*. Canberra, ACT: Australian National University Press, pp. 291–302.

Bonanno, A., 2015. The political economy of labor relations in agriculture and food. In: A. Bonanno and L. Busch, eds, *Handbook of the international political economy of agriculture and food*. Cheltenham: Edward Elgar, pp. 249–263.

Brandth, B. and Overrein, G., 2013. Resourcing children in a changing rural context: fathering and farm succession in two generations of farmers. *Sociologica Ruralis*, 53(1), pp. 95–111.

Bryant, L., 2015. Honor bound. In: L. Bryant and K. Jaworski, eds, *Women supervising and writing doctoral theses*. London: Lexington Books, pp. 21–34.

Bryant, L. and Garnham, B., 2013. Beyond discourses of drought: the micro-politics of the wine industry and farmer distress. *Journal of Rural Studies*, 32, pp. 1–9.

Bryant, L. and Garnham, B., 2015. The fallen hero: masculinity, shame and farmer suicide in Australia. *Gender, Place and Culture*, 22(1), pp. 67–82.

Chronis, A., 2012. Between story and place: Gettysburg as tourism imagery. *Annals of Tourism Research*, 39(4), pp. 1797–1816.

Cloke, P., Marsden, T. and Mooney, P., eds, 2006. *Handbook of rural studies*. London: Sage.

Cresswell, T., 2004. *Place: a short introduction*. Malden, MA: Blackwell.

Davidson, J. and Milligan, C., 2004. Embodying emotion, sensing place: introducing emotional geographies. *Social and Cultural Geography*, 5(4), pp. 523–532.

de Certeau, M., 1984. *The practice of everyday life*. Berkeley: University of California Press.

Derrien, M.M. and Stokowski, P.A., 2014. Sense of place as a learning process: examples from the narratives of Bosnian immigrants in Vermont. *Leisure Sciences*, 36(2), pp. 107–125.

Edwards, J., Cheers, B. and Bjornlund, H., 2008. Social, economic and community impacts of water markets in Australia's Murray–Darling Basin region. *The International Journal of Interdisciplinary Social Sciences*, 2(6), pp. 1–10.

Elsner, J., 1994. From the pyramids to Pausanias and Piglet: monuments, travel and writing. In: S. Goldhill and R. Osbourne, eds, *Art and text in ancient Greek culture*. Cambridge: Cambridge University Press. pp. 224–254.

Fischer, H. and Burton, R.J., 2014. Understanding farm succession as socially constructed endogenous cycles. *Sociologica Ruralis*, 54(4), pp. 417–138.

Gill, F., 2013. Succession planning and temporality: the influence of the past and the future. *Time and Society*, 22(1), pp. 76–91.

Gutsche, J. and Robert, E., 2014. There's no place like home: storytelling of war in Afghanistan and street crime 'at home' in the *Omaha World Herald*. *Journalism Practice*, 8(1), pp. 65–79.

Halbwachs, M., 1992. *On collective memory*. Chicago: University of Chicago Press.

Hoelscher, S. and Alderman, D.H., 2004. Memory and place: geographies of a critical relationship. *Social and Cultural Geography*, 5(3), pp. 347–355.

Iftekhar, M., Tisdell, J. and Connor, J., 2013. Effects of competition on environmental buyback auctions. *Agricultural Water Management*, 127, pp. 59–73.

Johnston, B., 1990. *Stories, community and place: narratives from middle America*. Bloomington: Indiana University Press.

Kearns, R. and Collins, D., 2012. Feeling for the coast: the place of emotion in resistance to residential development. *Social and Cultural Geography*, 13(8), pp. 937–955.

Kyle, G. and Chick, G., 2007. The social construction of a sense of place. *Leisure Sciences*, 29(3), pp. 209–225.

Loch, A., Bjornlund, H., Wheeler, S. and Connor, J., 2012. Trading in allocation water in Australia: qualitative understandings of irrigator motives and behaviour. *Australian Journal of Agricultural and Resource Economics*, 56, pp. 42–60.

Manzo, L., 2003. Beyond house and haven: toward a revisioning of emotional relationships with places. *Journal of Environmental Psychology*, 23, pp. 47–61.

Massey, D., 2005. *For space*. London: Sage.

McManus, P., Walmsley, J., Argent, N., Baum, S., Bourke, L., Martin, J., Pritchard, B. and Sorenson, T., 2012. Rural community and rural resilience: what is important to farmers in keeping their country towns alive? *Journal of Rural Studies*, 28(1), pp. 20–29.

Milligan, M. 1998. Interactional past and potential: the social construction of place attachment. *Symbolic Interaction*, 21, pp. 1–33.

Ng, F., Wilson, L. and Veitch, C., 2015. Climate adversity and resilience: the voice of rural Australia. *Rural and Remote Health*, 15(4), pp. 1–13.

Nora, P., 1989. Between memory and history: les lieux de mémoire. *Representations*, 26, pp. 7–24.

Potter, E., 2010. The ethics of rural place-making: public space, poetics, and the ontologies of design. *Cultural Studies Review*, 16(1), pp. 14–26.

Probyn, E., 2004. Shame in the habitus. *The Sociological Review*, 52(2), pp. 224–248.

Relph, E.C., 1976. *Place and placelessness*. London: Pion.

Said, E., 2002. Invention, memory and place. In: W. Mitchell, ed., *Landscape and power*. Chicago: University of Chicago Press. pp. 241–259.

Sartore, G., Kelly, B., Stain, H., Albrecht, G. and Higginbotham, N., 2008. Control, uncertainty and expectations for the future: a qualitative study of the impact of drought on a rural Australian community. *Rural and Remote Health*, 8(3), p. 950.

Strang, V., 2004. *The meaning of water*. Oxford: Berg.

Strang, V., 2005. Common senses: water, sensory experience and the generation of meaning. *Journal of Material Culture*, 10(1), pp. 92–120.

Tuan, Y., 1968. *The hydrologic cycle and the wisdom of God: a theme in geoteleology*. Toronto: University of Toronto Press.

Tuan, Y., 1977. *Space and place: the perspective of experience*. Minneapolis: University of Minnesota Press.

Tuan, Y., 1991. Language and the making of place: a narrative-descriptive approach. *Annals of the Association of American Geographers*, 81, pp. 684–697.

Van Patten, S. and Williams, D., 2008. Problems in place: using discursive social psychology to investigate the meanings of seasonal homes. *Leisure Sciences*, 30(5), pp. 448–464.

van Vliet, J.A., Schut, A.G., Reidsma, P., Descheemaeker, K., Slingerland, M., van de Ven, G.W. and Giller, K.E., 2015. De-mystifying family farming: features, diversity and trends across the globe. *Global Food Security*, 5, pp. 11–18.

Verrinder, G. and Talbot, L., 2015. Rural communities experiencing climate change: a systems approach to adaptation. In: R. Walker and W. Mason, eds, *Climate change adaptation for health and social services*. Victoria: CSIRO, pp. 179–199.

Weedon, C. and Jordan, G., 2012. Collective memory: theory and politics. *Social Semiotics*, 22(2), pp. 143–153.

Wheeler, S., Bjornlund, H. and Edwards, J., 2012. Handing down the farm? The increasing uncertainty of irrigated farm succession in Australia. *Journal of Rural Studies*, 2, pp. 266–275.

Wilson, J.L., 2005. *Nostalgia: sanctuary of meaning*, Lewisburg, PA: Bucknell University Press.

Wilson, R.L., Wilson, G.G. and Usher, K., 2015. Rural mental health ecology: a framework for engaging with mental health social capital in rural communities. *EcoHealth*, 12(3), pp. 412–420.

Worster, D., 1985. *Rivers of empire: water, aridity, and the growth of the American West*. Oxford: Oxford University Press.

Young, J.E., 1990. When a day remembers: a performative history of *Yom ha-Shoah*. *History and Memory*, 2(2), pp 54–74.

Zetland, D., 2013. All-in-auctions for water. *Journal of Environmental Management*, 115, pp. 78–86.

4 Material sites/sights and spatialities of exclusion

> What people do with the affordances of particular objects is, in part, to co-produce visualities.
>
> (Rose and Tolia-Kelly, 2012, p. 4)

Introduction

The previous chapter examined how water is given meaning through local memories and narratives about water flows and uses over time. Memory, however, is also preserved and 'rests on ... anchorage in space' (Wachtel, 1986, p. 216) and through this process material sites become *sites of memory* (Nora, 1989). This chapter examines how the intertwining of materiality and memory in rural landscapes shape contemporary social imaginaries of place that work to configure and reconstitute social practices of exclusion. The site of our analysis or 'the anchorage in space' we focus on is the building which houses the Renmark Irrigation Trust (RIT) where decisions about water allocations and use are made, where water infrastructure planning occurs and where, in contemporary times, it has become a localised point of advocacy for local irrigators in relation to the state (see Chapters 3 and 5). This material site is a site of significance for its socio-political importance in Renmark and equally for its material presence in sandstone, mortar and corrugated iron – reflecting a material site of memory. According to Tilley (2006, p. 23):

> Artefacts permit people to know who they are by virtue of the fact that they assume specific forms and images in the minds of the viewer in a manner not possible to convey in words.

The material has cultural meanings and relationships extending beyond its physical presence (Tilley, 2006, p. 23). The RIT building as a colonial artefact with its distinctive boardroom hosts the water board meetings and validates and produces ongoing knowledges (e.g. Hoelscher and Alderman, 2004) about the patriarchal colonial past in which Renmark emerged as an irrigation community. We examine how the construction and interior of the RIT building integrates events and understandings, serving to make them appear self-evident, creating a world where irrigation constructs community primarily through economic markets. In this way, the physicality of the RIT 'preserves memories of the past but always in a selective manner, simultaneously erasing part of it' (Tilley, 2006, p. 24). In particular, a history of violent colonisation resulting in the murder of Indigenous peoples and dismissal of their ownership and connection to country is erased. Colonial heritage also left little space for women's agri-political inclusion in irrigation communities, and this exclusion continues to be reproduced via patriarchal dominance in community, state and national socio-politics. The RIT building as a site, which is an informal museum, heralds the importance of objects from colonial times and also obliterates the waves of migration from the 1950s to the present day from Southern Europe, Southeast Asia and the Middle East. It symbolises a static notion of place.

A strong thread woven throughout international academic scholarship on rurality, Indigenous and ethnic diversity is that rurality is often a symbol of white national identity (e.g. Agyeman and Spooner, 1997; Askins, 2009; Bryant and Pini, 2011; Holloway, 2004; Neal, 2002; Nelson and Hiemstra, 2008; Panelli et al., 2009). This body of work highlights the importance of interrogating the 'rural idyll' to make evident the ethnic and cultural diversity of rural places. Indeed, 'despite the veneer of cultural homogeneity, the countryside is – and always has been – a multicultural space' and in the Australian context has always been an Indigenous space (Panelli et al., 2009, p. 355). As Agyeman and Spooner (1997) in their influential article on 'whiteness' and British rural spaces have argued, the very concept of the rural imaginary is racialised. Taking up this challenge to reconceptualise these spaces, scholars have 'de-centred white ruralities' (Panelli et al., 2009, p. 356) making visible the contributions and experiences of ethnically diverse and Indigenous peoples (e.g. Askins, 2009; Holloway, 2004; Nelson and Hiemstra, 2008). This chapter similarly exhumes presences that have been marginalised or denied in rural space by using material culture to dig beneath the surface and uncover practices of exclusion. While geographers, anthropologists and historians have taken similar approaches to methodologically engaging in the built environment and its objects to understand the historical and political dimensions to place, few have done so in relation to water politics. Our aim is to make visible how contemporary contestations and meaning making about water intersect with the politics of location and the global interconnectedness of places (see Chapters 2 and 3). Further, we argue that using a material approach has enabled us to understand what has not been made visible in interviews with irrigators, activists and those who govern water trusts, that is, questions of who is being represented in water politics and whose voices lie at the margins (see Chapters 5 and 6).

This chapter extends local meanings of community to include women, Indigenous peoples and ethnically diverse groups to disrupt male and predominantly white Anglocentric meanings and practices around water governance. Academic literature is sporadic on this topic and mostly has focused on water politics between communities and the state as well as between nation states. We aim to extend knowledge about water politics to analyses of past and present conditions and contexts around settlement and water occurring at the 'local' level configured around the RIT.

Whilst the RIT is a local site imbued with local meanings and globally shaped influences, it is also a case study that brings to the fore analyses of intersecting historical and contemporary local and global conditions, which give rise to delimiting the rights of citizens to engage in consultations and decision-making about water in irrigation communities. Hence, like Geismar and Horst (2004, p. 6) we came to realise as researchers in the field that:

> the material world ('objects', 'things', 'artefacts' or immaterial entities that have been reified in relation to these categories) is not only an end point or 'object' itself of social scientific description, but may also be used as a crucial interpretative tool to understand the nature of society, as an active agent within the social relations we were studying.

We initially discovered the active social presence of the RIT when we first attended a meeting at the local water trust. As researchers, our bodies and our gaze entered these landscapes. It is our complex and multifacted interactions with landscape which emerged from our embodied encounters and were subject to later interpretation (Conradson, 2005, p. 338). Haraway's (1988; 2007) concept of the gaze brings further attention to heterogeneous histories, which become increasingly evident after an event (or for us research encounters) (Bryant and Livholts, 2015a, p. 185). For Haraway, the gaze, or our way of seeing, is situated in the context of our own lived histories. As such, our research engagement afforded multiple materialities – our bodies as politically gendered subjects, the sites of materiality and memory incorporated in the RIT and the photographs we produced of these sites to record what we saw to enable analyses of these sites/sights. Our analyses of RIT are based on two photographs; the first is of the exterior of the RIT building and the second is a spanning shot which captures the boardroom and the portraits that line the wall of the boardroom. These photographs were chosen as sites of analysis as they reflected our embodied experience of these spaces. Thus, our process of fieldwork and data analysis became a 'synthesis of the visual and the discursive' (Geismar and Horst, 2004, p. 7), drawing on theoretical understandings of materiality, visuality and place.

We begin the chapter by examining theoretical meanings of materiality to understand the interconnections between subjects and objects and then turn to the relationship between the visual and the material. We examine how we see and what we see in materiality in the context of our situatedness and academic gaze – examining site and sight. Our analyses focus on deciphering the power relations shaping resource allocation. We note absences in governance and consultation regarding water use at the local level. In particular, Indigenous people remain unrepresented in local water politics and there is a continued lack of representation of women and an involvement of some ethnic 'others' over 'others'.

Materiality

Materiality as a concept has received attention across multiple disciplines in the humanities and social sciences, including geography, history, arts, cultural studies and archeology. In relation to geography, in the late 1990s there was a call to 'rematerialise' social and cultural geography (Jackson, 2000). This rematerialisation essentially required a re-centring of physical or non-human forms invoking theorisations that explored the significance of 'things', whether they be human-made or naturally occuring, and things and their relation to the social, economic and cultural (e.g. Geismar and Horst, 2004; Tilley, 2006; Hall, 2006; Whatmore, 2006). The return to materialism in theoretical debates was inspired by a politics of materialism, that is, a movement away from the solely discursive and performative in understanding the social world, to accounting for the relational nature of matter and humans in shaping the political, social, cultural and economic (Rose and Tolia-Kelly, 2012, p. 2; see also Jackson, 1989; Whatmore, 2006).

Across diverse theories which analyse the material world, there are plural meanings of materiality which begin within Marxism and historicism (Marx, 1977) and in more recent times Latour's (1999) actor network theory, theories of nationhood and identity (e.g. Ahmed, 2004b) corporeal feminism (e.g. Grosz, 2001) and material cultural studies (e.g. Beaudry and Hicks, 2010). However, there are some common understandings about the relational nature of the material and social. As Geismar and Horst (2004, p. 5, original emphasis) argue, the relational matter of the 'material' and 'social' refers to:

> an understanding of how categories (e.g. subject/object) or entities (e.g. person/thing) work *in relation* to one another to produce further sets of relationships or understandings that at their broadest might be termed 'culture', 'society' or 'locality'.

This suggests that material forms have an active role in shaping the social.

Bender (1992, p. 752), in her influential article on Stonehenge, challenges us to think about objects as more than taken for granted and unchanging. In regard to nature, material forms may move in space and across time, may erode, disappear and change shape, colour and form. Similarly, human-made objects may change over time, and photographs are an example of an object that can change in colour and form. Black-and-white photographs can fade to sepia and this change alone can alter our interpretation and feelings about a photograph. Thus, objects are inscribed with past histories but are not merely representative of past experiences, sites or knowledge. The point is that nature and human-made objects engage with experience rather than simply reflecting it. Material items shape the social as they are embedded in political, economic and socio-cultural relations and are 'part of the process through which people are both created by, and creators of, the world they live in' (Bender, 1992, p. 752). It is through this relational process with subjects that objects gain agency (Tilley, 2006). Individual and collective bodies encounter, consume, sense and emotionally and viscerally experience the material. Embodied interactions with matter also provide media in which identities are constituted and reconstituted. As Tilley (2006, p. 23) argues, 'Artefacts [and nature] permit people to know who they are by virtue of the fact that they assume specific forms or images in the minds of the viewer in a manner not possible to convey in words'. For example, river flows shape social and economic sustainability and recreational pursuits but also identities associated with place that can be difficult to express through language. Hence, objects have a part to play in constructing subjects. In relation to human-made objects, monuments are exemplars of cultural material forms which, whilst commemorating an event, usually war, also maintain and preserve memory, evoke emotion and promote social values like sacrifice for the nation as a greater good (Beckstead et al., 2011; Grissom and Harvey, 2003). These objects derived from stone, brick and mortar are built for longevity, 'lest we forget'.[1] The memorial is a site of memory and an intentional aid to collective memory. Thus, as Hoskins (2001) has argued, human-made objects are made to act and change the world in some way or they would not be created and it is through this action that objects have agency. Anderson et al. (2006) extend our thinking about objects and agency by bringing to the fore the relationships between politics and matter. They posit:

> How can we acknowledge the ways in which multifarious matters (GM goods, ID cards ... biometric passports, CO_2 emissions, artworks) can be, have been and still are enrolled into all sorts of political projects, bound up with social inequality and exclusion, whilst *also* acknowledging the considerable potential of matter to act in confusing, multiple, unexpected ways (to have agency of its own)?
> (Anderson et al., 2006, p. 10, original emphasis)

Matter and politics, or matter and the social/cultural, suggest that matter does not simply reflect meanings or that it is static property open to singular interpretation or representation. Indeed, there is a whole genre of social theorising, namely non-representational theory (see Chapter 1), that seeks to examine 'how life precedes and exceeds representation' (Anderson et al., 2006, p. 15). The premises underlying non-representational theory include an engagement with social and cultural practices, the lived body and in particular its sensations and emotions, as well as human–non-human relations (Anderson et al., 2006). As Anderson et al. (2006, p. 15) so aptly state, non-representational theory grasps 'how human and non-human subjects are involved, intertwined, with the world before they represent that world to themselves or others'.

Understanding the relational nature of objects, nature and the social world brings forth new methodological depth to research on natural and social worlds and humans and objects. Relationality enables an *engagement* with materiality, that is, the potential for analysing objects as more than static things but as active agents – allowing for the dual agency of subjects and objects (Geismar and Horst, 2004, p. 6). This dual agency results in a co-constitution of visualities and materialities in material culture (Rose and Tolia-Kelly, 2012).

Materiality and power

The relational nature of objects and subjects is evident in what matter is made, privileged and how it is interpreted and remembered through an embodied politics of envisioning (Rose and Tolia-Kelly, 2012), or for Haraway (1988) 'the gaze'. The crucial question in examining the politics of envisioning is asking which things are made visible, how, and why. Therefore, analysis of material culture requires an interrogation of visuality as more than seeing and materiality as more than matter.

Rose and Tolia-Kelly (2012, p. 4) argue that:

> Embedded in the *Visuality/Materiality* approach ... is a concern with a situated eye, an attunement to the collective, multiple and embodied textures, sensibilities and productive meanings of the visual through the material, and vice versa.

An embodied politics of envisioning takes account of the situatedness of who is seeing, acknowledging that subject positions are embodied (Haraway, 1988). Therefore, the contours of envisioning are shaped by gender, class, race, sex, ethnicity, age and (dis)ability, which is constituted in specific socio-historic conditions. Consequently, there are possibilities and limits to what is seen and how it is seen (Ahmed, 2004a). Further, what is viewed 'varies depending on who is looking and what is valued' (Bryant and Livholts, 2015a, p. 182). Vision is multidimensional and shifting, with multiple ways of seeing by a subject but also by subjects across populations, shifting according to social meanings that constitute our multiple situatednesses (Haraway, 1988, p. 586). As Bryant and Livholts (2015b, p. 7) have argued:

> Whilst the politics of location includes how our bodies are marked by our past it also allows for the notion that our bodies are ongoing achievements (Hinchliffe, 2003) subject to shifting practices of privilege and subordination.

What we see and is made visible is situated, as Rose and Tolia-Kelly (2012) clarify, in networks of hierarchies and discourses of power. The relations of power that shape what matter 'matters' have been extensively examined in social and cultural geography, illustrating the power dynamics that allow the interests of some to be served over others, thereby demonstrating that matter plays an important role in shaping collective subjectivities (e.g. Bakker and Bridge, 2006; Hall, 2006; Lefebvre, 1991). Hall (2006), for example, examined official celebrations and ceremonies in Cape Town, noting the privileging of Portuguese heritage and re-enactment of Portuguese settlement and at the same time the erasure of black South African culture. There is power inherent in the symbolic meanings attached to buildings, objects, photography and art, which shape place and power through the discourses which give precedence to these forms of matter over others. Thus, discourses around objects in place shape hegemonic discursive and embodied individual and collective histories and identities. As Tilley (2006, p. 23) aptly states:

> material forms may act as key metaphors of embodied identities, tools with which to think through and create connections around ... [to] articulate notions of personal identity with wider social notions of national character and soul ... Their efficacy as material metaphors is inseparable from bodily, sensory engagement with particular places.

These cultural material forms over time give hegemonic meanings to place and identities associated with place. However, these meanings which are created are selective, allowing some material forms and narratives of place to be remembered and celebrated and others to be excluded and forgotten (Tilley, 2006). As Hall (2006) reminds us, there are contested understandings, forms of resistance and reconstitutions of meanings of material culture in place that a singular and fixed account of buildings, monuments and objects allows us to neatly overlook. The situatedness of our gaze shapes place and gives meaning to material culture, reinforcing that our view is always partial and fragmented.

Sites/sights of visuality

The cultural material sites we use in this chapter to examine place-making images of inclusion and exclusion were those that captured our attention as non-locals, caused us to want to know more or caused a profound sense of discomfort. There was no objective choosing of sites, no weighing up of historical significance or controversy associated with the sites. The building, the black-and-white portraits and the heavy wooden furniture were chosen as items to photograph because they made an impression on us in the context of the place in which we found ourselves as researchers. They exuded a formality and elitism that had corporeal implications, that is, where to sit, how to sit and how to behave. This formality seemed incongruous to the landscape of scorching dry heat and the opaque and seemingly still Murray River. Moreover, the upright formal portraits and rich furnishing bespoke of wealth, belying the financial pain experienced in the district due to Australia's 'Big Dry' (the drought of 2001–2011).

There was an emotional and sensory impact, or as Pink (2006; 2009) would suggest, the visual and tangible cues enabled the emotional and the sensory to emerge. As research is multisensory and an embodied process, the senses, like knowledge and experience, shape what the researcher thinks, sees, feels, hears, smells and consequently interprets and analyses (Pink, 2009). For Mason and Davies (2009) visual objects open up the possibility for the 'tangible and intangible aspects of sight, sound, touch but also sensory imagination based on memory and future expectations' (Bryant, 2015b, p. 12). Thus, as embodied researchers we deem it important to include alongside analyses of interviews and water policies the sensory which shaped our understanding of physicality, social living conditions and water politics. Photographs are used in our analysis as they can carry or evoke 'information, affect and reflection particularly well' in ways that words alone may not (Rose, 2007, p. 238). Noting, in the vein of Haraway (2007, p. 585, original emphasis) that 'vision is *always* a question of the power to see', we acknowledge that what we see emerges from our situatedness. Our vision is partial and fragmented, influenced by academic knowledges and experiences. Hence, analyses are informed by our subjective reading of histories, our feminist and rural scholarship which shapes interpretations of presences and absences in the landscape. As Rose and Tolia-Kelly (2012, p. 3, original emphasis) eloquently state, 'this is research as *practices* (and methodologies) which remember that the politics of *doing* the visual are as material as matter is visual and that both are engaged beyond the ocular'. Our purpose of inquiry is to disrupt and connect objects geographically in and beyond the boundaries of place to make sense of inclusion and exclusion in 'water' or 'river' rural places that through discourse alone can be obscured. We are engaged in a practice of '(geo)politics of embodied, material encounter and engagement' (Rose and Tolia-Kelly, 2012, p. 3).

68 *Sites/sights and spatialities of exclusion*

In this chapter we analyse two photographs. The first is the building of the Renmark Irrigation Trust (Figure 4.1), the second is the Trust's boardroom and in particular, the furniture and the photographs lining the walls of the boardroom (Figure 4.2). As we have argued, sense of place is derived from our senses as well as our perceptual memories and knowledges, mediated by the present (Rose, 2007). As such, while 'Landscapes have an unquestionably material presence ... they come into being only at the moment of their apprehension by an external observer, and thus have a complex poetics and politics' (Cosgrove, 2006, p. 50). Each photo elicited meanings for us as researchers based on our academic knowledge about gender, race and power, and embodied sensory responses informed our interpretations when on-site but also post-site (Rose, 2007). Hence, the photos were first analysed individually by observing and then writing notes about our emplaced sensory experiences. Following this process we shared and discussed our interpretations and experiences using 'validity checkpoints' (Leavy, 2009, p. 19) to reach consensus about our theoretical interpretation of the visual data.

Materiality, visuality and exclusions

Ahlers and Zwarteveen (2009, p. 410) challenge us to examine discourses and politics about water access and use, suggesting that these 'hide political choices of distribution through naturalising, universalising and objectifying abstractions' and these abstractions may cause binaries between the natural and the social, thereby leaving social inequity and exclusion unmarked. In this section, through examination of aspects of cultural materiality, we decipher the power relations shaping resource allocation, noting who is absent in decision making about water use in the community under investigation, also noting that these same populations remain on the margins of water governance and management across the globe (Ahlers and Zwarteveen, 2009; Bressey, 2009; Earle and Bazilli, 2013).

The Renmark Irrigation Trust

The colonial past of the district of Renmark is made visible in the photograph of the Renmark Irrigation Trust building (Figure 4.1). The stone building, built in 1893 in colonial style and encircled by wide verandas, was built to administer the water supply to local growers and to govern the settlement.

It was not until 1960 that the district council distinguished itself from the Trust by setting up a new town council to govern Renmark. The centenary sign on the front of the building is centred to immediately catch the eye, boasting of the building's longevity. The gold plated sign etched in glass above the door, accompanied by a brass plate, acknowledges the building's

Sites/sights and spatialities of exclusion 69

Figure 4.1 Renmark Irrigation Trust building

purpose in a manner that reflects age and commands respect. The corrugated tin roof locates the building as particularly Australian.

Figure 4.2 shows the boardroom located in the Renmark Irrigation Trust building and captures the presence of chairmen of the Board dating from 1894 to 2012.

The oldest portrait is of Colonel C.M. Morant, heralded as first chair of the RIT, who incidentally was uncle to Harry 'Breaker' Morant, known for being court-martialed for the 'Eight Boers' case in which it was alleged that Boer POWs were shot. Breaker Morant is famous in folklore for being allegedly unfairly tried and executed by the British military eighteen hours after sentencing. The bar of the local pub in Renmark is named after Breaker Morant and the Morant story has become enmeshed within local folklore in Renmark.

The boardroom is dominated by large portraits of men in black and white, hung in heavy wooden frames which surround the small oblong shaped room. All the photographs are headshots of men dressed formally in suits. The formality of the photographs does not reflect their labouring bodies in horticultural industries. The heavy dark furniture fills the space. The sheer weight of the chairs makes them immovable. Their weight and dark tones cause the presence of these objects to be equally heavy and dominating – oppressive. The chairperson's chair is larger than the rest – almost a throne. The furniture is most likely English or German, carved of mahogany with dark red leather seating: furniture of a bygone era and distinctly a colonial import into the eucalypt, bold skied landscape of the Riverland. As we sat in these chairs addressing the board of RIT our discomfort was visceral, emotional and tangible. It was an affective experience occurring from the

Figure 4.2 Renmark Irrigation Trust boardroom

sensations of a body in a seat, a relation between a human and an object. As Anderson (2006, p. 736, original emphasis) suggests, affect is 'pre- and post contextual, pre- and postpersonal ... and [arising from] ... processual logic of *transitions* that take place during spatially and temporally disturbed encounters'. In this instance, this artefact provoked feelings of oppression which Tilley (2006) has suggested permitted us to know who we were through their form. Why our bodies felt out of place made sense to us in retrospect. History in the present was claiming in unequivocal terms that we had no right to sit in this space and what we were feeling but unable at the time to articulate were layered and multiple exclusions – the right to this space was created for white men. As women, we felt a sense of also being trapped in a place in which our bodies were foreign. It was not possible to move one's chair from the table or to leave the room when the space was filled with board members, all of whom were men, past and present. Indeed, there is a 120-year history of only male board members. Our bodies were out of place in this white male space. Hence, what matter matters in this space is that which celebrates white male colonisation of Renmark. In the RIT boardroom there is an intersection of the material and visual, culminating in a politics of material culture. This politics is exhumed by what we see, that is, our politics of location (Ahmed, 2004a) and the politics of history and place that renders which objects and people are made visible (Smith and Wiest, 2005). Hence, a co-constitution of visuality and materiality comes into being and as Rose and Tolia-Kelly (2012, p. 1) suggest this is the 'politics present in the everyday material world'. Analysing the RIT building and its boardroom as material spaces is an important process of 'exhuming of the ghosts and the places they inhabit ... to attempt to recover histories' (Bressey, 2009, p. 387).

Exhuming ghosts: women and water

Irrigation properties are not solely male-run enterprises. Whilst there are corporate properties in Renmark, the majority of properties are either owned or managed by families. There is a well-established, well-trodden path in the academic literature which underscores women's contribution to farming. This literature spans localities like Renmark and more broadly Australia, including other economies in the global north and demonstrates women's involvement in agricultural labour, accruing income, providing domestic labour, raising children, undertaking the accounting and banking and providing the financial and social resources for family succession (e.g. Brandth and Haugen, 2000; Bryant, 1999; Bryant and Pini, 2009; Saugeres, 2002; Shortall, 1994). However, the ownership of water rights by irrigators in Australia and elsewhere is largely a masculine affair that 'submerges a normative masculinity that underpins economic globalization', in particular in agricultural production (Davidson and Stratford, 2007, p. 1).

The idea that water is a feminist issue is not new and an extensive body of research exists which focuses on 'developing' countries and women's access and transportation of water (e.g. Cleaver and Hamada, 2010; Kevaney et al., 2013). In relation to poor and vulnerable women, accessibility to safe water is threatened, and internationally there has been a call for human rights based legislative change to protect the global commons as well as pragmatic changes to increase women's roles in leadership and management of water (Kevaney et al., 2013). Laws of nation states generally do not reflect women's engagement with water despite there being an international demand to include women in all aspects of water management (Earle and Bazilli, 2013; Gender and Water Alliance, 2006; International Fund for Agricultural Development, 2007).

Ahlers and Zwarteveen (2009, p. 410) have argued that water policies affect gender relations, and internationally there are 'feminist water agendas' that require addressing, in particular in relation to women's inclusion on water boards. They argue that whilst the inclusion of women on water boards is necessary, this approach will not be effective unless the board's engagement of women is more than tokenistic. This lack of representation is despite rural women in countries like Australia, Norway, the United Kingdom, Canada and the United States of America forming collectives in the late 1990s to give themselves voice(s) in agri-political arenas (Liepens, 1998). Women remain largely absent from debates and discussion on water in local communities and are in the minority in agri-committees, which influence legislative and policy changes around water resource allocation. In part, women's absence in the sphere of water politics is explicable in relation to their lack of representation in relation to men across all agri-political spheres. As Pini (2008) claims, globally women hold approximately 13 per cent of board membership and board positions in agriculture. Thus, despite women entering agri-political spaces since the 1990s, internationally men dominate across those spaces

(Pini, 2008). In specific relation to the Murray River and water governance, Alston and Mason (2008, p. 217) found that, across the spectrum of boards and committees set up to govern water at the national, state and local levels, exceptionally few women were in positions as chairs or commissioners of water commissions and trusts. At the time of their study in 2008 only one of seven water commissioners was a woman.

Zwarteveen's (2008; 2011) pioneering work shifts academic focus from the lack of representation of women in irrigation governance to critiquing the visibility of men. She has argued that the:

> discursive invisibility of men and masculinity in irrigation, has important political dimensions ... the source and workings of it remain hidden, in analogy with the watcher in the Panopticon prison whose controlling techniques importantly depend on his own invisibility.
>
> (Zwarteveen, 2008, pp. 111–112)

Masculine power is woven through multiple spaces and sites of irrigation including settlement, governance and professionalism. The colonisation of space and building of empire and nation through the lens of a frontier imaginary which imposes an ordering of land and water is a performance of hegemonic white masculinity. Similarly, the professionalisation of the irrigation engineer who was and remains overwhelmingly male and whose development of technologies exemplified modernity and progress sustained hegemonic masculine identity(ies), reinforcing technological prowess and power (Laurie, 2005; Zwarteveen, 2008). Zwarteveen (2008, p. 117) has argued that:

> Throughout the second half of the twentieth century, professional irrigation languages and identities become increasingly globalized and universal: irrigation engineers in Egypt, France, Australia the United States and the rest of the world tended to view the world in the same mathematical terms and the hydraulics of irrigation channels and the mechanics of dam construction were also the same whether applied in California or elsewhere.

She goes on to say that this global professionalisation of irrigation engineering 'not only helped to consolidate a particular epistemic tradition, but were also instrumental in establishing a global brotherhood of irrigation engineers' (Zwarteveen, 2008, p. 117).

The RIT boardroom represents these past masculine histories with the chairman of the Board, Chaffey, projecting his gaze upon those who sit in the boardroom and the display cabinets bearing witness to past pumping and water quality technologies. Bryant and Jaworski (2012), writing about the interrelationships between rurality, gender and work, bring attention to how the work of rural governance remains the domain of men. Organisations like RIT and other water trusts embody gender in organisational structures, practices and processes (Acker, 1990; 1998). Who is deemed suitable to be recruited to govern on water boards is influenced by 'the gender and race of existing jobholders [who] at least partially define who is suitable' (Acker, 2006, p. 449). As Bryant and Jaworski (2012) have argued, whilst inequality regimes are constructed by 'surrounding society, its politics, history, and culture' (Acker 2006, p. 443), they are also reconstructed at the scale of place. Similarly, Sultana (2009) has argued that gendered water relations are best understood via embodied subjectivities that take into account spatialities.

In more recent times, water and gender has been given increasing attention in the global north (O'Reilly et al., 2009). However, whilst this literature begins to critique the production, consumption, management, regulation, marketisation and decentralisation of water – this work remains in the minority and is still in its infancy. Much is yet to be learned about 'how experiences, discourses and policies of water are gendered, and how gender is created through processes of engagement, access, use and control of water resources' (O'Reilly et al., 2009, p. 381). We take up the apposite points made by water and gender scholars like Zwarteveen (2008; 2011) and Sultana (2009) that water politics is inextricably linked to gender politics, global politics of gender and water and politics of place.

Recovering histories: Indigenous absence/presence

The erasure of Indigenous presence is evident in Renmark's local history and this erasure is evident in this account:

> Although there were other white settlers in the area prior to their arrival the Chaffey Brothers are honoured as founders of Renmark. The Canadian born George and William Chaffey were invited to Australia to create an irrigation colony at Mildura [a nearby town] ... 30,000 acres from Bookmark Station lease was granted to the Chaffeys on which to build the new colony.
> (Renmark Paringa Information Centre, 2015)

The Australian rural idyll reflected in countless poems, songs and stories erases Indigenous presence and ownership (Bryant and Pini, 2011). In the 1960s and 1970s Australian children were taught to recite almost unthinkingly 'I love a sun burnt country, a land of sweeping plains' (Mackellar, 1904), a poem which implicitly assumes a landscape barren of human habitation. Indigenous people are absent in settler mythologies of the Australian outback which are 'rooted in heroic stories of settlement in adversity, and celebrate a process of transformation or celebrate a colonial taming of the land for economic productivity and white habitation' (Prout and Howitt, 2009, p. 396; see also Bunce, 2003; Gill, 2005; Waitt et al., 2007).

The RIT preserves a colonial 'heritage' that 'constructs "racial others" in ways that marginalize them from the norm' (Bressey, 2009, p. 389). The norm in this case is an understanding of Renmark as the first irrigation settlement in Australia established by the Chaffey Brothers who were invited from California to develop irrigation channels to enable the Riverland to become a region where fruit crops could be grown to service Australian commodity markets. This story of settlement is a sharing of technological development from one new world nation to another. It is a story of a new colony where white men control nature to build a 'progressive' place where families will reside, where communities become established, encouraging trade along the Murray River and the economic growth of the state and the nation. Prout and Howitt (2009, p. 396) refer to this narrative of settlement as 'frontier imagineries' that work to marginalise, silence, erase and deny Indigenous presence in its entirety, including cultural, emotional and physical affiliations by Indigenous people to country. Today there are approximately 600 people identifying as Indigenous living in the Riverland region of South Australia (total population 35,000) (Willis et al., 2004). Indigenous bodies in Australia are 'always out of place', neither urban nor rural and only authentic in wilderness spaces (Prout and Howitt, 2009, p. 396). Indigenous cultures in Australia are often treated within policy as homogeneous despite diversity in language, culture and customs (Langton, 2003; Onus, 2003). As Bryant and Pini (2011, p. 22) remind us, there is 'complex diversity within Indigenous cultures in the same rural regions (as well as across regions)'.

Across Australian rural places there is a sharing of similar historical narratives of 'settlement' rather than colonisation. In other 'new world' continents similar 'frontier imaginings' shape Indigenous exclusion – the United States of America, New Zealand and Canada, for example, are cases in point (White, 1994). Native American, Dakelh First Nation peoples from British Columbia and Maori peoples were cast in stories of settlement as non-productive with notions of a frontier or rural idyll which 'point[ed] to the selective and frequently hegemonic meanings of rural life ... based on predominantly agrarian populations' (Panelli et al., 2009, p. 357).

Taming of country and productivity continues to resonate in Australian narratives of agriculture, and Bryant and Garnham (2015) have shown that farming ideology marks farmers as heroes and battlers, working for the good of the nation in the context of drought. Drought in Australia is constituted as a 'white' problem affecting the livelihood of farmers which also has the capacity to erode Australian country towns. However, in rural New South Wales and other areas of Australia, drought has resulted in Indigenous people losing their livelihood (Rigby et al., 2011). Many Indigenous men in particular are employed on farms and as these become economically threatened labouring jobs are reduced.

Australian Indigenous histories and culture are deeply connected to rural spaces. For many Indigenous peoples in Australia the term 'country/ies' refers to an ontological connection to all that encompasses landscape, that is, water, hills, mountains, earth, plants, rock formations and so on. These elements have meanings that link family and kin, language and customs, identity, spirituality and understandings of past, how to care for country and live in the present (Bergson et al., 2004; Rose, 2004). As Shaw et al. (2006, p. 270) have argued, the concept of land is 'a key point on which Global north and Indigenous world views have historically diverged'. White configurations of country in academic and public discourse and policy marginalise or absentise Indigenous peoples (Suchet, 2002). The pursuit of Native Title first recognised in Australian courts in 1992 enabled Indigenous peoples to formulate extensive and complex legal claims to reclaim their country, or indeed, parts of it (Cunliffe, 2007). This reclamation emerges from colonisation, causing country and home to be 'an "intensely political site"' (Blunt and Dowling, 2006, p. 188) enmeshed in the invasion and occupation of Indigenous land (Bryant and Pini, 2011, p. 29). Attempts to resolve Native Title often place Indigenous communities in lengthy legal conflict with the state, potentially with other Indigenous groups and mining and agricultural interests (Cunliffe, 2007). In this legal framework the onus is on Indigenous peoples to prove custodial ownership (Cunliffe, 2007.

From the white gaze, Indigenous relationship to country is often coupled with rurality to promote tourism (Waitt, 1999) and progress the discourse of the noble savage, a culture of antiquity or more frequently as something exotic, worthy of the fleeting white gaze (Carter and Hollinsworth, 2009; Ramzan et al., 2009). Contrastingly, in the media and in political statements and policies Indigenous rural and remote communities are discursively constituted as 'dysfunctional', plagued by substance abuse and an inability to care for their children (Behrendt, 2007; Slater, 2008). The previous prime minister of Australia, Tony Abbott, has suggested that Indigenous communities in remote areas be closed, denying resources of water, electricity and services to these communities, giving no heed to the traditional owners of the land and their cultural heritage and affiliation with country. Indeed, to the present day European colonisation shapes Indigenous peoples' experiences in Australia as there remains no treaty with traditional owners. Australian Indigenous history and heritage lies at the surface of meanings of rurality. More often than not, Indigenous presence is reflected in place names, feeding the construction of Indigenous as exotic. In terms of governance of rural communities Indigenous people are rarely present on boards, councils or committees unless rural communities are remote and predominantly Indigenous. Carter and Hollinsworth (2009) suggest that Aboriginal people are denied full citizenship rights and are rarely afforded opportunities to economically and socially develop and conserve rural places. In regard to water planning, especially in times of water scarcity, Indigenous people are inadequately consulted (Nikolakis and Grafton, 2014; Wirf et al., 2008). Indeed, whilst national policy has been drafted to incorporate Indigenous cultural values into water planning and management, in reality this has been ineffective, failing to examine the value Indigenous groups give to water and ecology (Jackson et al., 2012). In relation to Indigenous meanings associated with the Murray River, a Ngarrindjeri elder in his report to the Murray–Darling Basin Commission (2002, p. 7, cited in Willis et al., 2004, p. 187) explained:

> The land and waters is a living body. We the Ngarrindjeri people are part of its existence. The land and waters must be healthy for the Ngarrindjeri people to be healthy. We are hurting for our country. The Land is dying, the River is dying, Kurangk (Coorong) is dying and the Murray Mouth is closing. What does the future hold for us?

Willis et al. (2004, p. 189) consulted Indigenous groups from the Riverland about their concerns regarding water use, conservation and cultural relationships to water. They found that fishing stock had declined and that people were concerned about the natural flows of the Murray being disturbed either through flood or drought impacting on eco-systems.

The constitution of Aboriginal bodies as always out of place has resulted in 'configurations of post-colonial and neo-colonial governance [with] Indigenous access to and use of resources ... [being] obliterated or severely eroded and controlled by external institutional systems' (Panelli et al., 2009, p. 359; see also Nakata, 2003). Legislation on Indigenous rights to water varies across Australian states and territories (Poirier and Schartmueller, 2012). Whilst different Acts provide variable access and consultation regarding water allocation and use, commonly 'Aboriginal water rights are secondary to state granted other rights' (Poirier and Schartmueller, 2012, p. 321).

However, to include Indigenous peoples on water boards will require an acceptance of Indigenous knowledges about the river eco-system, which in turn may challenge the state and those irrigators who are driven by an economic determinism to access as much water as is required to produce their crops despite weather conditions.

Ethnicities in and out place

The white rural idyll also denies and at times rejects the presence of ethnic diversity, promoting specific white identities (Holloway, 2004; Rogaly, 2008). In an Australian context, non-Anglo/Celtic/Germanic groups are often excluded from social and political networks (Bryant and Pini, 2011; Missingham et al., 2006). As Panelli et al. (2009, p. 357) argue, 'rurality perpetuates a privileged whiteness that serves to exclude not just non-White groups, but also minority White groups who are imagined as "not-quite" White'.

Returning to the RIT building, as women working in Academe we have experienced feelings of bodily transgression (Bryant, 2015a) but feeling ill at ease in our bodies at the RIT was more than a reflection of our own gendered lived experience. The room, the portraits and the furniture filling the space were markedly unusual in the context of the landscape of Renmark and the Riverland as we had experienced it. The RIT building and boardroom were 'disconnected from contemporary sites of rurality' (Bressey, 2009, p. 389). The built landscape of Renmark and the people who move in it are a visible testament to the diversity of cultures who have played a part in shaping this place. Driving into the township in this flat landscape the domed structure of the Greek Orthodox church is visible in the main street and located a few streets away is one of the few rural mosques in South Australia. Since the 1950s Renmark has been a district made up of many cultures and presently there are several generations of Greek, Italian, Indian, Southeast Asian and Turkish Australians living in the area. Residing in Renmark today there are over thirty-one different ethnic groups (ABS, 2011).

The Trust building and its boardroom are constructed spaces that reify the past in what is a culturally diverse rurality. As Jordan et al. (2009, p. 376) argue, 'white discourses have been entrenched despite the fact that rural areas in most global north countries do have a long-standing immigrant history', which also leaves unacknowledged that Renmark and the Chaffey brothers, like all white settlers, were indeed immigrants. Understanding rural places as both porous and mobile opens up the possibility for social relations that stretch in and beyond place. As Massey suggests (1994, pp. 21–22) place can be understood as a 'meeting place' and:

> imagined as particular articulations of these social relations, including local relations 'within' the place and those many connections which stretch way beyond it. And all of these are embedded in complex, layered histories. This is place as open, porous, hybrid – this is place as meeting place.

Massey's conceputalisation of place brings forth the historical and ongoing global, national and local inflows and outflows of migration and the changing social relations which accompany them. Askins (2009, p. 366) uses a similar theorisation and deploys the concept of transrurality to 'reposition ... [white rurality] as a site within multi-cultural, multi-ethnic, transnational and mobile social imaginaries'. Rural landscapes in the global north alter with each successive wave of immigration as cultural heritages are expressed in the built environment (Jones et al., 2009). Indeed, what buildings are built and where they are located is an ongoing part of the contestation of rural space informed by questions of belonging and tensions around insider and outsider status (Hayden, 1995). However, visibility of ethnic diversity in the landscape is not necessarily synonymous with acceptance and equality in rural places in relation to citizenship rights about development and deployment of natural resources (Helzer, 2001). There is limited scholarship which examines from an Australian perspective ethnic diversity, water governance and water rights along the Murray–Darling Basin.

The RIT is clearly a testimony to a patriarchal colonial past but its building and boardroom is also a living colonial and patriarchal space. Indigenous peoples, women of all cultural origins and some ethnically diverse groups remain unrepresented on the water board. These are present practices of exclusion. However, the 'other' is not simply excluded; some 'other' voices are more inclined to be heard. As Askins (2009, p. 365, original emphasis) argues, 'ethnic minorities were perhaps too easily written *as* excluded "rural others"'. Similarly, Little (1999, p. 438) has suggested that referring to groups as 'othered' 'implies a static treatment of that individual and group identity'. In relation to the RIT board, ethnically diverse groups of men are increasingly represented on the board, especially those whose cultural group was represented in earlier waves of immigration. Therefore, as Holloway (2004) and Smith (1993) have claimed, the category of 'racialised rural other' is not static or easily bounded, suggesting that dominant discourses work to position people as 'in or out of place in different spaces' (Holloway, 2004, p. 155). The exclusion of ethnically diverse groups from some rural spaces has meant in many countries that the so called 'other' resists, challenges and changes the rural landscape to include new materialities where places of worships, clubs or sports, festivals and customs are introduced to claim physical, cultural and emotional space (Jordan et al., 2009). Moreover, there is a temporal as well as a spatial unevenness in the claiming of space. For example, Jordan et al. (2009) in their study of Griffith in New South Wales, which shares similar commodity development and migration settlement patterns to Renmark, show the development of built meeting places and in particular Italian clubs at different times to accommodate the cultural diversity across the population of Southern and Northern Italians. The work of Jordan et al. (2009, p. 377) shows how 'successive waves of immigrants have transformed the rural landscape through the construction of public and private spaces, expressing their cultural heritage by altering their physical environment'. However, there has been little academic focus until recently on the heritage sites built by more recent waves of migrants (in Australia post-1900s) to rural areas (e.g. Dunn, 2003; Lalich, 2003). Indeed, according to Jordan et al. (2009, p.

377) these sites remain out of sight due to 'official definitions of heritage that prioritise "elite" or "Global north" heritage at the expense of places significant to marginalised cultural groups'. Official definitions of heritage exemplify the relational nature of the material and social and typify what is made visible as culture in and beyond rural communities.

The built environment also illustrates the contextual and shifting nature of rural power relations and questions of exclusion and belonging. It underscores that whilst in some ways material culture appears fixed like the RIT building itself, resistance and reconstitution of meanings of material culture nevertheless occur (Hall, 2006). In some contexts 'othering' and exclusion occur alongside the agency of ethnically diverse groups and individuals shaping rural landscapes. What remains unknown and lacking in our account of ethnicities and materiality are the discursive and sensory responses to the RIT of culturally diverse groups. Lived experiences may well reconstitute that space as archaic and irrelevant or alternative spaces of resistance may be created to engage in water politics, which take into account diverse cultural experiences and needs in growing horticulture in the Riverland. Further, assuming ethnic groupings as homogeneous, consensual and un-fractured, sharing similar aims for water allocation and use in the district is equally problematic. This is true particularly given widespread diversity amongst landholders in the Riverland in relation to the scale and size of their enterprises, new machinery purchase, hiring of managers and labourers, forged relationships and knowledge through longevity in the district.

Conclusion

Water politics in local places are shaped by past histories that bleed into present day politics. The historic socio-political conditions of the RIT as the first Australian water trust demonstrate movement across global spaces, shaping models of irrigation and community governance around water and the constitution of place and questions around belonging. As a material site, the RIT, its colonial building and boardroom, are a living formal museum, reproducing settlement narratives about taming nature and channeling water flows for economic and social productivity. Centring the RIT as a material site of memory enabled an examination of the relational nature between the material and subjects in shaping current water practices, especially around inclusions and exclusions in relation to water governance. The RIT building challenges an interpretation of space as simply representational, and our presence in that space as researchers enabled us to begin the process of examining the intertwining of embodied sensations associated with place with the materiality of place. Our embodied discomfort enabled an analysis of objects as more than static things bringing to light visuality, causing us to question what is made visible in the RIT building and its boardroom and why (Geismar and Horst, 2004). Visual objects allowed the possibility of tangible and intangible dimensions of sight, sound, touch and sensory imagination to be realised (Mason and Davies, 2009). Hence, power relations inherent in this material site came into being in relation to our sight.

Materiality and photography were useful methodologically to elicit power dynamics based on gender, race and ethnicities, which shape water allocations and management. It is unlikely that traditional qualitative research methods like interview data would have brought forth the diverse historical and socio-political dimensions of water use and governance in the Riverland. As Rose suggests, visual methodologies evoke 'information, affect and reflection – particularly well' (2007, p. 238) in ways that words may not (Russell and Diaz, 2011, p. 2). Materiality and visuality brought insight into how matter is involved in political projects that extend, shift and are shaped through time.

The recovering of histories and absences and presences in Renmark as an irrigation community illustrated a distinct lack of consultation and involvement in governance for women, Indigenous peoples and some ethnic groups in local and national water politics. Women remain either unrepresented or under-represented on water boards and committees, consultation with Indigenous people remains patchy across Australian states and territories, and in relation to ethnic diversity, those with greater longevity in rural districts are more likely to be involved in official governance.

Engagement with bodies of international literature shows a lack of academic interrogation of exclusions and visibilities in water management. The literature to date focuses on 'developing' countries with limited examination of especially women's engagement and the engagement of ethnically diverse groups in global north economies. Water politics in the community of Renmark and more broadly, across global north countries, is shaped by what knowledges are made visible, and these largely remain masculinised and the province of 'white' men. As Panelli and others (2009) have argued, it is time to de-centre white masculine constitutions of the rural, recognising heterogeneity. In relation to water politics we would argue that it is now imperative to recognise heterogeneity and practice heterogeneous engagement in water governance.

Note

1   'Lest we forget' is a phrase often employed to remember soldiers who have died in war and stems from Rudyard Kipling's poem, 'The Recessional'. It is also often used on headstones of soldiers in Australia and is read out at the end of the Anzac Day speech during the official Anzac Day (25 April) celebrations.

References

Acker, J., 1990. Heirarchies, jobs and bodies: a theory of gendered organizations. *Gender and Society*, 4(2), pp. 139–158.

Acker, J., 1998. Hierarchies, jobs, bodies: a theory of gendered organizations. *Feminist Foundations: Toward Transforming Sociology*, 3, p. 299.

Acker, J., 2006. Inequality regimes gender, class, and race in organizations. *Gender and society*, 20(4), pp. 441–464.

Agyeman, J. and Spooner, R., 1997. Ethnicity and the rural environment. In: P. Cloke and J. Little, eds, *Contested countryside cultures: otherness, marginalisation, and rurality*. London: Routledge, pp. 197–217.

Ahlers, R. and Zwarteveen, M., 2009. The water question in feminism: water control and gender inequities in a neo-liberal era. *Gender, Place and Culture: A Journal of Feminist Geography*, 16(4), pp. 409–426.

Ahmed, S., 2004a. *The cultural politics of emotion*. Edinburgh: Edinburgh University Press.

Ahmed, S., 2004b. Declarations of whiteness: the non-performativity of antiracism. *Borderlands* (e-journal), 3(2). Available at: www.borderlands.net.au/index/html (Accessed 15 June 2014).

Alston, M. and Mason, R., 2008. Who determines access to Australia's water? Social flower, gender, citizenship and stakeholder priorities in the Australian water crisis. *Rural Society*, 18(3), pp. 214–219.

Anderson, B., 2006. Becoming and being hopeful: towards a theory of affect. *Environment and Planning D*, 24(5), pp. 733–752.

Anderson, B., Cook, I. and Maddern, J., 2006. 'Geography and matter/materiality'. Workshop series sponsored by the RGS (IBG) Social and Cultural Geography Group.

Askins, K., 2009. Crossing divides: ethnicity and rurality. *Journal of Rural Studies*, 25, pp. 365–375.

Australian Bureau of Statistics, 2011. 2011 Census community profiles. Available at: www.censusdata.abs.gov.au/census_services/getproduct/census/2011/community profile/SSC40615?opendocumentandnavpos=220 (Accessed 23 December 2014).

Bakker, K. and Bridge, G., 2006. Material worlds? Resource geographies and the 'matter of nature'. *Progress in Human Geography*, 30(1), pp. 5–27.

Beaudry, M.C. and Hicks, D., eds, 2010. *The Oxford handbook of material cultural studies*. Oxford: Oxford University Press.

Beckstead, Z., Twose, G., Levesque-Gottlieb, E. and Rizzo, J., 2011. Collective remembering through the materiality and organization of war memorials. *Journal of Material Culture*, 16(2), pp. 193–213.

Behrendt, L., 2007. The emergency we had to have. In: J. Altman and M. Hinkson, eds, *Coercive reconciliation: stabilise, normalise, exit Aboriginal Australia*. North Carlton, VIC: Arena Publications, pp. 15–20.

Bender, B., 1992. Theorising landscapes, and the prehistoric landscapes of Stonehenge. *Royal Anthropological Institute of Great Britain and Ireland*, 27(4), pp. 735–755.

Bergson, H., Paul, N.M. and Palmer, W.S., 2004. *Matter and memory*. Mineola, NY: Dover Publications.

Blunt, A. and Dowling, R., 2006. *Home*. London and New York: Routledge.

Brandth, B. and Haugen, M., 2000. From lumberjack to business manager: masculinity in the Norwegian forestry press. *Journal of Rural Studies*, 16(4), pp. 343–356.

Bressey, C., 2009. Cultural archaeology and historical geographies of the black presence in rural England. *Journal of Rural Studies*, 25, pp. 386–395.

Bryant, L., 1999. The detraditionalization of occupational identities in farming in South Australia. *Sociologia Ruralis*, 39(2), pp. 236–261.

Bryant, L., 2015a. Honor bound. In: L. Bryant and K. Jaworski, eds, *Women supervising and writing doctoral theses*. Lanham, MD: Lexington Books, pp. 21–34.

Bryant, L., 2015b. Introduction: taking up the call for critical and creative methods in social work research. In: L. Bryant, ed., *Critical and creative research methodologies in social work*. Surrey: Ashgate Publishing, pp. 1–26.

Bryant, L. and Garnham, B., 2015. The fallen hero: masculinity, shame and farmer suicide in Australia. *Gender, Place and Culture*, 22(1), pp. 67–82.

Bryant, L. and Jaworski, K., 2012. Minding the gaps: examining skill shortages in Australian rural non-agricultural workplaces. *Journal of Management and Organisation*, 18(4), pp. 499–515.

Bryant, L. and Livholts, M., 2015a. Memory work and reflexive gendered bodies: examining rural landscapes in the making. In: B. Pini, B. Brandth and J. Little, eds, *Feminisms and ruralities*. Lanham, MD: Lexington Books, pp. 181–194.

Bryant, L. and Livholts, M., 2015b. Opening the lens to see, feel and hear: using autoethnographic textual and visual methods to examine gender and telephony. In: L. Bryant, ed., *Critical and creative research methodologies in social work*. Surrey: Ashgate Publishing, pp. 109–130.

Bryant, L. and Pini, B., 2009. Gender, class and rurality: Australian case studies. *Journal of Rural Studies*, 25(1), pp. 48–56.

Bryant, L., and Pini, B., 2011. *Gender and rurality*. New York: Routledge.

Bunce, M., 2003. Reproducing rural idylls. In: P. Cloke, ed., *Country visions*. Harlow: Pearson Education, pp. 14–28.

Carter, J. and Hollinsworth, D., 2009. Segregation and protectionism: institutionalised views of Aboriginal rurality. *Journal of Rural Studies*, 25(4), pp. 414–424.

Cleaver, F. and Hamada, K., 2010. 'Good' water governance and gender equity: a troubled relationship. *Gender and Development*, 18(1), pp. 27–41.

Conradson, D., 2005. Landscape, care and the relational self: therapeutic encounters in rural England. *Health and Place*, 11, pp. 337–348.

Cosgrove, D., 2006. Modernity, community and the landscape idea. *Journal of Material Culture* 11(1/2), pp. 49–66.

Cunliffe, E., 2007. Anywhere but here: race and empire in the Mabo decision. *Social Identities*, 13(6), pp. 751–768.

Davidson, J. and Stratford, E., 2007. En(gender)ing the debate about water's management and care: views from the Antipodes. *Geoforum*, 38(5), pp. 815–827.

Dunn, W.N., 2003. *Public policy analysis: an introduction*. New York: Pearson Higher Education.

Earle, A. and Bazilli, S., 2013. A gendered critique of transboundary water management. *Feminist Review*, 103(1), pp. 99–119.

Geismar, H. and Horst, H.A., 2004. Materializing ethnography. *Journal of Material Culture*, 9(1), pp. 5–10.

Gender and Water Alliance, 2006. Synthesis report of the Gender and Water Alliance at the Fourth World Forum, 16–22 March, Mexico. Gender and Water Alliance Secretariat, Dieren, the Netherlands.

Gill, N., 2005. Aboriginal pastoralist, social embeddedness, and cultural continuity in Central Australia. *Society and Natural Resources*, 18(8), pp. 699–714.

Grissom, C.A. and Harvey, R.S., 2003. The conservation of American war memorials made of zinc. *Journal of the American Institute for Conservation*, 42(1), pp. 21–38.

Grosz, E., 2001. A thousand tiny sexes: feminism and rhizomatics. In: C. Boundas and D. Olkowski, eds, *Gilles Deleuze and the theater of philosophy*. New York: Routledge, pp. 187–210.

Hall, M., 2006. Identity, memory and countermemory: the archaeology of an urban landscape. *Journal of Material Culture*, 11(1/2), pp. 189–209.

Haraway, D., 1988. Situated knowledges: the science question in feminism and the privilege of partial perspective. *Feminist studies*, 14(3), pp. 575–599.

Haraway, D., 2007. *When species meet*. Minneapolis: University of Minnesota Press.

Hayden, D., 1995. *The power of place: urban landscapes as public history*. Cambridge, MA: MIT Press.

Helzer, J.J., 2001. Old traditions, new lifestyles: the emergence of a Cal-Ital landscape. *Yearbook of the Association of Pacific Coast Geographers*, 63(1), pp. 49–62.

Hinchliffe, R., 2003. People, plants and performance: on actor network theory and the material pleasures of the private garden. *Social and Cultural Geography*, 4, pp. 99–113.

Hoelscher, S. and Alderman, D.H., 2004. Memory and place: geographies of a critical relationship. *Social and Cultural Geography*, 5(3), pp. 347–355.

Holloway, S., 2004. Outsiders in rural society? Constructions of rurality and nature–society relations in the racialisation of English gypsy-travellers, 1869–1934. *Environment and Planning D: Society and Space*, 21, pp. 695–715.

Hoskins, B.J., 2001. Modelling of the transient eddies and their feedback on the mean flow. *Large-scale Dynamical Processes in the Atmosphere*, 1, p. 169.

International Fund for Agricultural Development, 2007. *A summary of IFAD's strategic framework 2007–2010*. United Nations: IFAD.

Jackson, P., 1989. *Maps of meaning: an introduction to cultural geography*. London: Unwin Hyman.

Jackson, P., 2000. Rematerializing social and cultural geography. *Social and Cultural Geography*, 1, pp. 9–14.

Jackson, S., Tan, P.L., Mooney, C., Hoverman, S. and White, I., 2012. Principles and guidelines for good practice in Indigenous engagement in water planning. *Journal of Hydrology*, 474, pp. 57–65.

Jones, H.G., Serraj, R., Loveys, B.R., Xiong, L., Wheaton, A. and Price, A.H., 2009. Thermal infrared imaging of crop canopies for the remote diagnosis and quantification of plant responses to water stress in the field. *Functional Plant Biology*, 36(11), pp. 978–989.

Jordan, K., Krivokapic-Skoko, B. and Collins, J., 2009. The ethnic landscape of rural Australia: non-Anglo-Celtic immigrant communities and the built environment. *Journal of Rural Studies*, 25, pp. 376–385.

Kevaney, K., Siebel, M., Hyde, K. and Nazer, D., 2013. Water, women, waste, wisdom and wealth: harvesting the confluence of opportunities. *International Journal of Cleaner Production*, 60, pp. 4–10.

Lalich, W., 2003. Ethnic community capital: the development of ethnic social infrastructure in Sydney. Doctoral dissertation, University of Technology, Sydney.

Langton, M., 2003. Introduction: culture wars. In: M. Grossman, ed., *Blacklines: contemporary critical writing by Indigenous Australians*. Carlton, VIC: Melbourne University Press, pp. 81–91.

Latour, B., 1999. On recalling ANT. In: J. Law and J. Hassard, eds, *Actor network theory and after*. Oxford and Malden, MA: Wiley, pp. 15–25.

Laurie, N., 2005. Establishing development orthodoxy: negotiating masculinities in the water sector. *Development and Change*, 36(3), pp. 527–549.

Leavy, P., 2009. Fractured femininities/massacred masculinities: a poetic installation. *Qualitative Inquiry*, 15(9), pp. 1439–1447.

Lefebvre, H., 1991. *The production of space*. Oxford: Blackwell.

Liepens, R., 1998. 'Women of broad vision': nature and gender in the environmental activism of Australia's 'women in agriculture' movement. *Environment and Planning A*, 30(7), pp. 1179–1196.

Little, J., 1999. Otherness, representation and the cultural construction of rurality. *Progress in Human Geography*, 23(3), 437–442.

Mackellar, D., 1904. *My country*. Available at: www.dorotheamackellar.com.au/archive/mycountry.htm (Accessed 23 April 2015).

Marx, K., 1977. *Selected writings*. D. McLellan, ed. Oxford: Oxford University Press.

Mason, J. and Davies, K., 2009. Coming to our senses? A critical approach to sensory methodology. *Qualitative research*, 9(5), pp. 587–603.

Massey, D., 1994. *Space, place and gender*. Cambridge: Polity Press.

Missingham, B., Dibden, J. and Cocklin, C., 2006. A multicultural countryside? Ethnic minorities in rural Australia. *Rural Society*, 16(2), pp. 131–150.

Nakata, P.A., 2003. Advances in our understanding of calcium oxalate crystal formation and function in plants. *Plant Science*, 164(6), pp. 901–909.

Neal, S., 2002. Rural landscapes, representation and racism: examining multi-cultural citizenship and policy-making in the English countryside. *Ethnic and Racial Studies*, 25(3), pp. 442–462.

Nelson, L. and Hiemstra, N., 2008. Latino immigrants and the renegotiation of place and belonging in small town America. *Social and Cultural Geography*, 9(3), 319–342.

Nikolakis, W.D. and Grafton, R.Q., 2014. Fairness and justice in Indigenous water allocations: insights from northern Australia. *Water Policy*, 16, pp. 19–35.

Nora, P., 1989. Between memory and history: les lieux de mémoire. *Representations*, 26, pp. 7–24.

Onus, L., 2003. Language and lasers. In: M. Grossman, ed., *Blacklines: contemporary critical writing by Indigenous Australians*. Carlton, VIC: Melbourne University Press, pp. 92–96.

O'Reilly, K., Halvorson, S., Sultana, F. and Laurie, N., 2009. Introduction: global perspectives on gender-water geographies. *Gender, Place and Culture: A Journal of Feminist Geography*, 16(4), pp. 381–385.

Panelli, R., Hubbard, P., Coombes, B. and Suchet-Pearson, S., 2009. De-centring white ruralities: ethnic diversity, racialisation and Indigenous countrysides. *Journal of Rural Studies*, 25, pp. 355–364.

Pini, B., 2008. *Masculinities and management in agricultural organizations worldwide*. Aldershot: Ashgate.

Pink, B., 2006. *Socio-economic indexes for areas (SEIFA): technical paper*. Canberra, ACT: Commonwealth of Australia.

Pink, B., 2009. *10 year book of Australia*. Canberra, ACT: Australian Bureau of Statistics.

Poirier, R. and Schartmueller, D., 2012. Indigenous water rights in Australia. *The Social Science Journal*, 49, pp. 317–324.

Prout, S. and Howitt, R., 2009. Frontier imaginings and subversive Indigenous spatialities. *Journal of Rural Studies*, 25(4), pp. 396–403.

Ramzan, B., Pini, B. and Bryant, L., 2009. Experiencing and writing Indigeneity, rurality and gender: Australian reflections, special edition, edited by Ruth Panelli, Phil Hubbard, Brad Coombes and Sandie Suchet-Pearson, de-centring white ruralities: ethnicity and Indigeneity. *Journal of Rural Studies*, 24(4), pp. 435–443.

Renmark Paringa Information Centre, 2015. *Renmark Paringa: SA's river paradise*. Online. Available at: www.visitrenmark.com (Accessed April 2015).

Rigby, C.W., Rosen, A., Berry, H.L. and Hart, C.R., 2011. If the land's sick, we're sick: the impact of prolonged drought on the social and emotional well-being of Aboriginal communities in rural New South Wales. *Australian Journal of Rural Health*, 19, pp. 249–254.

Rogaly, B., 2008. Intensification of workplace regimes in British horticulture: the role of migrant workers. *Population, Space and Place*, 14(6), pp. 497–510.

Rose, G., 2004. 'Everyone's cuddled up and it just looks really nice': the emotional geography of some mums and their family photos. *Social and Cultural Geography*, 5, pp. 549–564.

Rose, G., 2007. *Visual methodologies: an introduction to the interpretation of visual materials*. London: Sage.

Rose, G. and Tolia-Kelly, D.P., 2012. Introducing a manifesto for practice. In: G. Rose and D.P. Tolia-Kelly, eds, *Visuality/materiality*. Surrey: Ashgate Publishing, pp. 1–12.

Russell, A.C. and Diaz, N.D., 2011. Photography in social work research: using visual images to humanize findings. *Qualitative Social Work*, 12(4), pp. 1–21.

Saugeres, L., 2002. The cultural representation of the farming landscape: power, masculinity, nature. *Journal of Rural Studies*, 18(4), pp. 373–384.

Shaw, W.S., Herman, R.D.K. and Dobbs, R., 2006. Encountering Indigineity: re-imagining and decolonising geography. *Geografiska Annaler B*, 88, pp. 267–276.

Shortall, S., 1994. Farm women's groups: feminist or farming or community groups, or new social movements? *Industrial and Labor Relations Review*, 28(1), pp. 279–291.

Slater, L., 2008. Aurukun, we're happy, strong people: Aurukun kids projecting life into bad headlines. *Borderlands e-journal*, 7(2), pp. 1–14. Available at www.borderlands.net.au/vol7no2_2008/slater_aurukun.pdf (Accessed 15 May 2015).

Smith, J. and Wiest, D., 2005. The uneven geography of global civil society: national and global influences on transnational association. *Social Forces*, 84(2), pp. 621–652.

Smith, S.J., 1993. Bounding the borders: claiming space and making place in rural Scotland. *Transactions of the Institute of British Geographers*, 18, pp. 291–308.

Suchet, S., 2002. 'Totally wild?' Colonishing discourses, Indigenous knowledges and managing wildlife. *Australian Geographer*, 33(2), pp. 141–157.

Sultana, F., 2009. Fluid lives: subjectives, gender and water in rural Bangladesh. *Gender, Place and Culture*, 16(4), pp. 427–444.

Tilley, C., 2006. Introduction: identity, place, landscape and heritage. *Journal of Material Culture*, 11(1/2), pp. 7–32.

Wachtel, N., 1986. Introduction: memory and history. *History and Anthropology*, 12, pp. 207–224.

Waitt, G., 1999. Naturalizing the 'primitive': a critique of marketing Australia's Indigenous peoples as 'hunter-gatherers'. *Tourism Geographies*, 1(2), pp. 142–163.

Waitt, G., Figueroa, R. and McGee, L., 2007. Fissures in the rock: rethinking pride and shame in the moral terrains of Uluru. *Transactions of the Institute of British Geographers*, 32(2), pp. 248–263.

Whatmore, S., 2006. Materialist returns: practicing cultural geography in and for a more-than-human world. *Cultural Geographies*, 13(4), pp. 600–609.

White, R., 1994. Frederick Jackson Turner and Buffalo Bill. In J. Grossman, ed., *The frontier in American culture: an exhibition at the Newberry Library, August 26, 1994–January 7, 1995*. Berkeley: University of California Press, pp. 7–67.

Willis, E., Pearce, M. and Jenkin, T., 2004. The demise of the Murray River: insights into lifestyle, health and well-being for rural Aboriginal people in the Riverland. *Health Sociology Review*, 13(2), pp. 187–197.

Wirf, L., Campbell, A. and Rea, N., 2008. Implications of gendered environmental knowledge in water allocation processes in central Australia. *Gender, Place and Culture*, 15(5), pp. 505–518.

Zwarteveen, M., 2008. Men, masculinities and water powers in irrigation. *Water Alternatives*, 1(1), pp. 111–130.

Zwarteveen, M., 2011. Questioning masculinities in water. *Review of Women's Studies*, 46(18), pp. 40–48.

5 Riskscapes

Introduction

As the materiality of sites and sights recording histories of water governance shift over time, so does water as a material form. Changing water flows and water scarcity through prolonged drought, poor management and unequal access exacerbate social relations and claims to water access and use. The water politics which emerge from changing water allocations are enmeshed in relations of risk, trust and uncertainty. This contested sphere becomes highly politicised and fraught as governments, water trusts and interest groups attempt to intervene through legislation or advocacy by altering water allocations within communities.

In relation to the irrigation communities of the Riverland and Central California, whilst the states in question constitute discursive constructions of drought, irrigators construct a different discourse – a discourse of water allocation. These are fundamentally different constitutions of risk with significantly different outcomes to those envisaged by policy makers and legislators. The Riverland and Fresno provide situated case studies of local responses, conditions and contexts and thus, situated knowledges (Haraway, 1988). Whilst there are global understandings shared across geographic locations, how these are interpreted, rejected, reworked and utilised is situated in place within the context of local politics at both the state and community levels.

The politics of drought are an intrinsic part of the interstices between socio-cultural interactions with land and water, which reshape land/waterscapes into riskscapes. Riskscapes act as a terrain where risk construction is an interweaving constellation of knowledges and imaginaries and is lived in multiple ways in spatial contexts (Müller-Mahn, 2012; November, 2008). Within riskscapes subjects negotiate, move between and experience risk differently and unequally. Moreover, riskscapes are mapped on the body as much as they are located in spaces and places. Hence, risk is not only perceived and imagined but is visceral and emotional. While risks are materially experienced in the context of limited water supplies, they are also emotionally experienced as a threat to livelihood and as fear and anger associated with litigious action. Risks and threats are also experienced as emotional connections to water and landscape or provoked through fighting for the right for one's voice to be heard.

We use the concept of 'riskscapes' to examine relations of risk and understand how risks are given meaning by multiple subjects, experienced and contested in the Riverland and Central California. Three inter-related themes emerge from our analyses, illustrating how risks are spatially revealed, mediated, managed, contested and lived. The first theme examines relational meanings of risk, uncovering how meanings emerge and are used to mitigate against risk. The spatial and local dimensions of risk become apparent in the context of the histories of mobilisation by irrigators to shape water allocation. Water allocation is discursively constituted as a right tied to land ownership and thus, the second theme focuses on multiple discourses of individualisation which shape knowledges about water and its place in the market and community. The final theme considers institutional trust/distrust in relation to governmental policy and how governments are rendered as objects, which exacerbate the 'rights' of the individual. Hence, the question of regulation of risk for irrigators is often at odds with the neo-liberal subject that individually manages risk.

From risks to riskscapes

Studies on risk have been informed by the seminal work of Beck (1992) and Giddens (1992), who argued that in late modernity society has been transformed to a 'Risk Society'. Late modernity has a set of distinct features associated with risk in which modern technologies can exceed prediction and control (Beck, 1996). Uncertainty, they suggest, derives in part from constant changes in social structures, requiring individuals to choose between numerous and often competing alternatives to insure against the presence of risk. Earlier conceptualisations of risk understood it as calculable through rational decision-making in which, properly understood, risk could be reasonably managed (Beck, 1996). However, the body of scholarship on risk that was developed in the 1990s and early 2000s challenged the idea that risk is a static, knowable entity. This literature defined risk in multiple ways, arguing that it is constructed or manufactured (Beck, 1992; Lash, 2000), porous, discursively constituted, embodied and lived (Adam and Van Loon, 2000; Lash, 2000). However, to theorise risk as constructed does not suggest risks are immaterial. As Adam and Van Loon (2000, p. 2, original emphasis) explain:

> we argue for the need to understand risk construction as a practice of manufacturing particular uncertainties that may have harmful consequences to 'life' in the broadest sense of the term. The essence of risk is not that it is happening, but that it *might be* happening. Risks are

manufactured, not only through the application of technologies, but also in the making of sense ... one cannot, therefore, observe a risk as a thing-out-there – risks are necessarily constructed.

This is a notion of risk where risk becomes revealed as latent, invisible, contingent and harming (Adam and Van Loon, 2000, p. 2). The point that risk becomes revealed implies knowledge and interpretation (Beck, 1992). In terms of risk and the environment, Szersznski (1999, p. 240) suggests that:

> late modern risks are also highly mediated risks, extremely open to social definition and interpretation. This generates a politics of knowledge in which different social groups continually compete over risk definition.

Hence, questions of power, politics and social location will shape what is determined as risk, which opens up possibilities for polarising and contentious 'definitions' but also gives power to specific knowledges over others. For example, as Chapter 4 indicated, Indigenous knowledges about water flows and risk to the environment are given less credence in Australia and elsewhere than those of governments or irrigators. What risk is and the way it is discursively constituted, engaged with and legitimised (or delegitimised) has consequences for how water institutions govern, which water allocation practices are set in place and the environmental management and intervention programs implemented.

These porous complexities of defining and thereby, for communities, living with risks suggest that risk associated with the same phenomena may be constituted differently within and across communities. In this way, risk is socio-historic and thereby situated and cultural (Lash, 2000), subject to 'relations of risk-definitions' (Adam and Van Loon, 2000, p. 2). Understanding risk as shaped by relations enables the theoretical and empirical emergence of multiple definitions that are constituted in relation to other knowledges, practices, ideologies and values and mediated institutionally for example by the media, think tanks and research centres.

Building on this sociological body of work on risk, geographers have recently contributed to theorising spatiality and risk using Actor Network Theory (Müller-Mahn, 2012; November, 2008). This literature ostensibly brings together conceptualisations of space and risk, and in doing so uses the term 'riskscapes'. Müller-Mahn uses the concept of riskscapes to:

> indicate how individual actors and social groups develop personal visions of risk and translate them into spatial settings. The notion of 'riskscapes' has a metaphoric meaning that combines the idea of territory or a landscape with that of risk.
>
> (Müller-Mahn, 2012, p. xxiii)

In this way, Müller-Mahn links materiality and meaning where risks 'as a structuring phenomena' shape landscape into riskscape (2012, p. xxiii). November (2008) draws our attention to symbiotic relationships between risk and space and how these transform each other. Using Latour's (1999) Actor Network Theory (ANT), contemporary risk theorists trace 'the assemblage and interaction chain between technical artefacts, natural substances and human organisation and disorganisation' (Neisser, 2014, p. 4). Following ANT methodologies, November empirically demonstrates that 'categories of risk are not fixed, but rather move in relation to events' (November, 2008, p. 1525). She provides an example of a flood that occurred in a region where a village was not mapped as at risk of flood, thereby revealing a new category of risk. This new category had consequences in rethinking the spatial contours of the village and putting new infrastructure in place to assist drainage. Thus, November (2008, pp. 1525–1526) is arguing that risks are *actant* and play a role in transforming the collective. It is in this regard that we take up the idea of risk in relation to water scarcity as embedded within multiple and shifting local meanings and actions that materially, culturally, socially and economically alter communities and community relations. At the same time, the local shapes and is shaped by national and global debates about the impact of climate change and drought, ways of reducing water scarcity and debates about water rights and governance. This chapter reveals how risk is given meaning and operates at the local level to shape community relations. We particularly find synergies with Beck and Kropp's (2011, p. 4) idea that relations of risk definition and management are continually constituted and reconstituted at multiscalar levels but, importantly, locally through everyday interactions, commodity groups, disputes, forms of activism and media.

Risk and trust

Trust is a concept that works in parallel with risk. In the water politics literature trust is understood as a medium for regulating perceptions of risk and uncertainty between and across individuals and institutions (e.g. Candlin and Crichton, 2013; Cook, 2003; Lewis and Weigart, 2012; Rosa et al., 2013). Bachmann and Zaheer (2006) have shifted the theoretical focus from Beck's 'Risk Society' to a 'Trust Society', in which individuals actively seek out a basis for the development of trust to safeguard their own well-being. Such trust helps to alleviate uncertainty by transferring perceived risks to another individual or institution. Hence, Bachmann and Zaheer (2006) suggest it is the identification of the *perception* of risk which is important. It is this conceptualisation of risk which departs from Beck's (1992) now widely criticised assertion that risk has increased and is less calculable (Elliot, 2002). Instead, rather than being increased or inherent, Higgins (2001) suggests risk may be governed, brought into the realm of 'knowing' through specific strategies that highlight and define events as 'risky', such as the identification of drought through particular discourses of governance. In part, the perception of risk, and by association the operationalisation of trust, occurs based on the confidence one places in another actor or institution's motivations.

Risk, trust, regulation and power

Regulatory institutions play a critical role in constituting risk and also in enabling trust among irrigators and water governing boards (Bryant and George, 2016). The social dynamics of trust inform riskscapes, shaping local understandings and response to risk. In this section we examine the concept of institutional trust, drawing on the scholarship of Fukuyama (1995) and Möllering (2006). Fukuyama (1995) and Möllering (2006) have argued that to trust an institution there must be a consistency to the functions and rules of the organisation which provide a basis for expectations, shared cultural meanings, habitual performances and regular procedures. According to Fukuyama (1995, pp. 26–27), trust is established, in part, by the 'spontaneous sociability' fostered by organisations which create affiliations within them and foster business relationships which grow the larger community involved.

More recently, the literature on trust has also turned attention to *regulatory trust*, in which the operations of bodies of power are examined to better understand how issues of risk, control, dependency, and power are negotiated between institutions and social actors (Bratspies, 2009; Hedgecoe, 2012; Pautz, 2009). Regulating bodies are understood to be operating under high levels of uncertainty, based on rapid changes in technology, public policies, and additionally within the water policy context, environmental and legislative shifts. In order to act effectively within these conditions, regulatory bodies rely upon a legitimation of their power through the processes of social trust, in which actors within the system recognise the inevitability of uncertainty and utilise previous experiences to build trust for favourable future outcomes (Bryant and George, 2016).

As per Foucault's (1998 [1976]) understanding, the 'power' discussed here is not a singular repressive sovereign power but instead includes the possibility of productive power, in which subjects and objects are constituted through discourse, and power relations are predicated on the legitimation of knowledge and expertise. Briefly, this conceptualisation of 'government' incorporates activities undertaken by any body or authority which utilises particular knowledges and practices to achieve a desired outcome (Dean, 1999). In addition to sovereign and disciplinary power, which utilise law and norms respectively to control and normalise particular behaviours, Foucault (1998 [1976]) suggests there also exists biopower, a form of governmentality which relies upon the abilities of individuals, in which the population is understood to be 'a pool of resources whose potential for self-optimisation needs to be unleashed' (Oels, 2005, p. 19). Through this form of governmentality, the market is made central, and the subject is responsible for transforming themselves into a competitive individual who makes calculated and effective decisions in order to compete effectively. Thus, the autonomy of agents within the system is simultaneously enabled and constrained, as this system of governmentality delineates the field of opportunities within which the subject may act, in part constituting the agent as an already subjugated subject who may act 'freely' but only when they act in ways prescribed by the system.

Implicitly then, as Foucault (1998 [1976]) suggests, the development of trust relies upon power, in which risk is made governable through expertise and historical processes of legitimation which suggest that the institution possesses the ability to control risk in a way that individuals are not able to, or believe they are not able to, and thus individuals are prompted to rely primarily on the institution rather than themselves. These feelings of vulnerability due to risk position the individual in an 'asymmetrical relationship' with the institutions in whom they place their trust, further legitimating the power of the institution through the desire for certainty (Candlin and Crichton, 2013, p. 2).

We argue that this framing of power and governmentality provides an important lens through which to make sense of irrigators' perceptions and decision-making. Governmentality highlights the expectation that irrigators would have performed at optimal levels within an individualised system, but to do so they must have made multiple decisions which then increase feelings of risk and uncertainty. In turn, they attempt to ameliorate risk and uncertainty through the expertise of an institution – in Renmark's case via the RIT, and in Fresno through a gaining of power by criticising environmental lobbyists. This understanding of the trust/risk dynamic, and particularly regulatory trust/risk, provides an effective conceptual basis upon which to examine relationships between key players in water politics, raising questions about the contexts and conditions in which trust is given or withheld.

Relational risks

The construction and reconstruction of risks as relational are embedded in local meanings and responses to mitigating risk. In both USA and Australian sites, risk is constituted in relation to non-irrigators and in particular governments and other divergent voices around water allocations and water rights. In Renmark, risk is mediated by placing trust in the RIT to advocate for irrigators and in Central California risk is mediated for some through lobbyists and wealthy irrigators. In this section we examine meanings and relations of risk, beginning with the RIT before turning to Central California to examine the centrality of capital in shaping water allocations, causing unequally distributed risk across riskscapes to other irrigators and community members. The Californian experiences especially illustrate risk and hazards as visceral, emotional and embodied.

In the Riverland, risk is largely revealed and defined in relation to two pressing issues for irrigators. The first involves uncertainty associated with the cost set for purchasing water and the second involves uncertainty about the percentage of water allocated by government for irrigation. Feelings of uncertainty about water prices were echoed in the following concerns by irrigators:

> we don't know ... see, no one knows what the market will do. If there is not much water around the price of water will go up. If there is a lot of water around the price will be cheaper.
>
> because you don't really know what is going on.

As Bratspies (2009) suggests, regulators who are identified as trustworthy provide the basis upon which the actors may participate effectively in social and economic systems through social cooperation. This has significant outcomes for institutions such as the RIT, whose position as a mediator between the community and other regulatory bodies relies upon a substantial level of trust from those irrigators who choose to participate in the system (Bryant and George, 2016). By trusting regulatory bodies to act on behalf of a larger group, the possible vulnerabilities of individual decisions whose cumulative effects may not be accounted for are ameliorated (Bratspies, 2009). However, regulatory trust of RIT to mediate market risk was not a universally held decision among RIT irrigators. Some irrigators suggested that the Murray–Darling Basin Plan (see Chapter 2) 'does provide certainty ... we need some sort of guarantee of the future water supply for growers, for horticulture, for the industry'. In this way, risks associated with the same phenomenon are constituted differently within the same group of irrigators – they are subject to 'relations of risk definitions' (Adam and Van Loon, 2000, p. 2). As Bjornlund et al. (2010) have noted, some irrigators became increasingly supportive of the market, enabling cost effective expansion and levels of water security.

The RIT, with the overwhelming support of the community, has advocated for its members in relation to government policies around water allocation and pricing. Advocacy has involved lobbying politicians, attending and being vocal at community consultation meetings, and submitting written feedback to government departments and government ministers. Advocacy by the RIT, especially during the time of drought, became a key focus of the institution and a central expectation of their members. Indeed, as members felt increasingly uncertain and powerless in relation to drought and national debates as to requisite water allocations, individual members allocated power and gave trust to the RIT to advocate on their behalf. Irrigators perceived that RIT's role was to give voice to community concerns and negotiate deals with government. As one irrigator suggested:

> I've expected they would be across all the issues and that they will communicate on to the growers how it affects them ... and that they would be making contingency plans to make sure that any adverse effects on the rate payers is reduced. I would hope they would go in and try and get the best deal for us.

Irrigators talked about trusting that the RIT had greater knowledge and was therefore well placed to invest one's trust in to advocate on their behalf to government. For example:

> they know better than me, I don't know how I'd go about it [advocating] and RIT in this community is a tier above the local council, they have their finger on the pulse.

Risk is being defined as limited knowledge to engage in advocacy but also as a limited knowledge and power in reading and responding to riskscapes which are inherently political (Müller-Mahn, 2012). The symbiotic relation between risk and space here is associated with the political contours of the MDB plan and its potential impact on South Australia, whose political position is understood by RIT members as inferior to Australian states positioned upstream (see Chapter 6).

The embeddedness of risk in local communities shapes relational meanings of risks but also shows that risks are emotional. The position that there was potential for fairness in water access through RIT was frequently reiterated in comments like 'RIT aim to get us a fair deal with water [allocations] in the future; water buy backs are a threat ... RIT are making our values known'. As Bryant and Garnham (2014) focusing on Australia and Price and Evans (2009) on the United Kingdom have argued, emotions have tended to be regarded as separate from the economic arena. In the same way neo-liberal transformation of the political economy of agriculture impacts on farmer distress (e.g. Bryant and Garnham, 2013; Price and Evans, 2009); risk, and especially threat, are heavily imbued with emotions that are informed by moral meaning (Lupton, 1992). Consequently, the expectation or hope for a 'fair deal' suggests an ethical expectation in sharing or diminishing risk. This hope for diminished risk is emotionally linked to feelings associated with anger and moral meanings associated with blame and injustice, or conversely, hope for recognition and justice (Barclay et al., 2005; Bryant and Garnham, 2014). The emotional inoperative content of risk and threat are embodied responses to risk and in this way, riskscapes mark the body. The reference to 'our values' by irrigators indicates a shared ethical position among RIT growers that implies an ethics of self and community care contouring this local riskscape. Moreover, ethics of self and community were represented in the belief of irrigators that the RIT was a collective body representing the community beyond the needs of its individual membership. An irrigator explained that:

> in order for them to deliver water effectively, it's going to have a rolling effect towards the town.

For irrigators, the position of trust was derived from the notion that the RIT could deliver a collective voice, informed by knowledge and values of the community (Bryant and George, 2016). Hence, trust was formed and developed through the legitimisation of the RIT as a 'knowing body' by its members. This knowledge created an 'identification-based trust', in which the actors were so well known that one may act for the other based upon their knowledge of what that individual wants (Lewicki and Bunker, 1996, p. 122). As a regulatory body, the RIT advocates for water allocations across its membership and as a body or collective can control for risk in ways that individual landowners are less able to (Foucault, 1998 [1976]). The RIT is situated as a trustworthy body as it has demonstrated to its members its ability to govern risk by *consistently* meeting the needs and expectations of the individuals involved over time (Bratspies, 2009), with irrigators identifying an appreciation that the RIT had 'stepped up' during the drought years.

> I've got a fairly safe guaranteed supply of water ... when I want that water I can get hold of it. That it's provided through a well maintained service so that it's not subject to outages for long periods of time. That it's available at a fair price, which I think the RIT does and again, like the administration and the management and the advocacy roles are all sort of taken care of as part of it.

In contrast, in Central California there was not a single 'knowing body' like the RIT advocating on behalf of 'the community' to increase water allocation, nor was there a collective advocacy and bargaining process with government. Advocacy for water rights was significantly contested and fragmented amongst different stakeholders. Risks were relationally defined in heterogeneous ways and some members of the community referred to the schism between farmers and developers on the one hand and environmentalists on the other, noting that water agencies lobbied on the basis of agricultural versus environmental discourses. For example, as a participant explained:

> the farmers and developers say 'We need more water, come on Northern California is swimming in water' and Northern Californians are saying

'You're killing the Delta, you're killing one of the great estuaries in the history of the world, do you know what you are doing?'

This narrative reveals risk to river health and economic development as a 'struggle between competing, alternative[s]' (Maseele, 2015, p. 7). This positioning of risk demonstrates the inextricable links between nature and society and reveals the environment as a political category (Maseele, 2015). The development of a body of scholarship termed 'political ecology', 'understood as the political economy of socio-environmental change' (Bakker, 2003, p. 36), encapsulates the role of the state and capital in shaping water use and allocations. In the context of California, political ecology has become marked as the drought has continued, with water politics becoming further fragmented and contested, with interest groups hiring lobbyists to influence Congress to receive greater access to water. The lobbying campaign has primarily been driven by owners of 'the 600,000 acres' of farmland in Fresno and Kings counties and the owners of Kern County-Paramount farms. For Fresno irrigators with smaller properties, there was a 'hope' that one could trust other irrigators accessing the same water supply, 'a hope that the big guy down the way doesn't drain everything down because you don't have the money to fight him in court so it's a situation of big growers, lots of money dominates' (Journalist). The hope that trust was possible is an ethical expectation and 'hope' signifies moral meanings about ethical conduct in relation to water use. Trust in the collective, however, is eroded by what is a capital intensive divide as individual interests are being advocated for and served. Another irrigator further explained how land was divided:

> On the west side of the valley there are now about 240 irrigators and about 40 control half the land. Dynastic clans ... [names an irrigator and his family] has about 300,000 acres and the government built a dam and that is state water they have access to.

The state water this participant is referring to is the large scale water project funded by government involving storage and movement of snowmelt from the Sierra Nevada mountains and the Delta to farmers (Balazs and Ray, 2014, p. 606). The result of conveying water to farmlands has meant that farmers receive 'unlimited surface water rights for agriculture, but 95 per cent of the Valley's residents ... receive groundwater for drinking' (Balazs and Ray, 2014, p. 606). Hence, whilst scholars have suggested that 'risk controversies as "risk conflicts" ... [involve] contestation between actors over conflicting risk definitions ... based on the confluence of competing epistemic and ideological disagreements' (Maseele, 2015, p. 7), this position fails to account for differences associated with capital–material differences that shape meanings of risk and ways to control or minimise risk. While there is unequal risk in relation to water allocations and continued productivity in times of drought across both sites, the concentration and centralisation of capital is more profound in shaping water allocation in California, leading to significant and more severe unequal distributions of risk.

Returning to a political ecology and unequal risks, risk associated with water in Central California extends beyond maintaining a profitable agricultural enterprise to the ecological, physical and social health of the broader community. The ground water accessible to San Joaquin Valley residents has been contaminated by agricultural inputs and by-products (Balazs and Ray, 2014). Participants identified multiple risks associated with poor water and air quality stemming from fertilisers and pesticides. A participant explained the impact on health:

> we have polluted groundwater ... we use more pesticides in this valley than anywhere else in the world, we use more fertiliser which has a lot of impurities in it ... we have the worst air quality in America and one out of six kids has asthma.
>
> (Activist)

Another participant described risks associated with high levels of nitrate in drinking water, informing us:

> There's more dairy cows than people in this county, there's like 400,000 people and there's like a million cows, there is no way to clean up the waste, it goes into these lagoons. Nitrates found in drinking water cause blue baby syndrome, which can be fatal, it's a fatal blood disease in some kids ... there are not documented cases because these people do not tell anybody. There has been cancer clusters here, two or three of them, the drinking water here is abominable. In fact, the United Nations came here two years ago in a worldwide tour through places like Zambia and seeing where water needed to be cleaned up. They came to Tulare County and looked at the water and said these conditions are deplorable.

The poor water quality in parts of Central California has been well documented in academic articles, government reports and the media, certainly since the 1970s to the present day. Balazs and Ray (2011, p. 607) have argued that when systems are not working, in particular regulatory systems, individuals and households take on 'the burden of mitigation'. However, this 'burden of mitigation' for poor water infrastructure, along with nitrogen-based fertilisers, is distributed unequally (Balazs et al., 2011; Morello-Frosch et al., 2001). It is left up to the individual to negotiate with water boards and:

In 2010, residents from the community of East Orosti testified to the United Nations Special Rapporteur on the Human Right to Water and Sanitation that, because they speak in English with Spanish accents, they were continually turned away by water board administrators when seeking clarification on their water quality reports.

(Balazs and Ray, 2011, p. 607)

A 2011 report by London et al. documented the inter-relationships between environmental risk and health risk in the San Joaquin Valley. They systematically demonstrated that the higher the social vulnerability, the greater the exposure and impact of environmental hazards, arguing that:

Nearly one-third of the nearly four million people in the region face both high degrees of environmental risks (for example, toxic air and water pollutants) and high degrees of social vulnerability (poverty, low levels of formal education, and low English literacy).

(London et al., 2011, p. 2)

These risks are embodied and lived. Disease from poor quality water infiltrates the body minimising autonomy over one's body and, indeed, water as a life source turns into risk. Through the state deploying risk, bodies 'become objects of self surveillance' (Bunton and Peterson, 1997, p. 7). Community members are trapped in a physical environment which they are unable to change and which they are unable to leave. A participant revealed that:

A lot of people want to leave the Valley because of the air quality, their kids have asthma, everyone is coughing all the time. And you know, those are the fortunate ones that can move away. [But] how do you move away, when you've got nothing, you've haven't got $2 to your name, where are you going to go? You can't even buy a ticket to anywhere. So I think the exploitation of the resource base of California led directly to the situation that we have in this valley today. Which is crime and poverty, bad health, bad water, bad air, a terrible education system, we are near the bottom in the US.

(Activist)

There has been an increasing focus in academic scholarship on questions of human rights and social justice in relation to risks associated with climate change and economic and social production and consumption and its impact on water and landscapes, broadly defined as environmental justice (e.g. Sze and London, 2008; Walker, 2009). More recently, the study of environmental justice has developed further, focusing on questions about spatiality and equity across national borders, the role of transnational corporations, production of risks and environmental hazards across borders and global collective problems like waste (Carmin and Agyeman, 2011). Schlosberg (2013) has suggested that environmental justice networks and academic study has moved from its traditional liberal frame of reference where justice was situated with the individual and is now focusing on the interstices between individual and communities and the interstices between human and non-human. As discussed in the introduction to this text, sociology and social and cultural geography have furthered understandings of environment and justice through theorisations of human and non-human (e.g. Braun and Castree, 1998; Castree, 2003; Dalby, 2007; Whatmore, 2003). In particular, as Whatmore (2003, p. 166) suggests, a 'permitting [of the] more promiscuous and volatile configurations of the social and the material that complicate the laboured divisions and rapprochements between culture and nature'. In relation to water rights in Central California, the interstices between human and non-human move us beyond a Marxist's thinking that 'capitalism materially remakes nature in its image' (Castree, 2003, p. 170). Rather, as Castree (2003, p. 180) suggests, the works of Marxists and structuralists in cultural geography can aid us by providing a 'relational approach to culture-nature but one where the material capacities are myriad, variable, lively and shared' and therefore a relational understanding of risk (see Chapter 4). At the same time, 'this approach would be sensitive to historical-geographical difference but would also look for the ways in which relations to nature are nonetheless consequentially ordered in a capitalist world' (Castree, 2003, p. 180). For Castree, this approach requires a critical analysis of the interstices between culture, nature and the economic. In the context of Central California, capital has shaped poor water and air quality and cultures of local governance have had minimal impact in changing these conditions. In this lengthy but demonstrative quote below a participant explained how culture, nature and socio-economic and political conditions intersect and work to diminish social and environmental justice. He explained:

> Well, they [the coal industry and the agricultural industry] were using the national wildlife refuge as a dumping ground for this toxic waste water from the fields in the Westland and it killed fish and birds and caused deformities … this trace element selenium did that and you will find selenium where there is fertilisers and where you mine for coal … I discovered selenium is native to the soil and shows up on the sea bed … when you irrigate the selenium in the soil it dissolves, goes into a solution. And then you have a wastewater because well underneath the valley soils, anywhere from 20 to 200 feet there are clay layers back from when this valley was a lake. And you know lakes slowly build up clays, and they're virtually impermeable or pretty close so when you irrigate, the water goes

down and hits the clay. And when they flood irrigating from above, it hits the clay back up to the root zone and because water is so salty it will kill the crop. So they had a plan to drain that water off the top layer and drop the water table below the root zone and then you have this waste water. Well, they used to think it was just sodium and sulphates and your generic salts, it sounded pretty harmless. What's also in there is arsenic, mercury, nickel, lead, molybdenum and selenium … they had a small river of waste … next thing its killing birds and fish … the government invested a billion dollars in this irrigation project and the growers screamed bloody murder that without drainage they can't farm, there's the horns of the dilemma which has faced us now for the last 30 years.

(Journalist)

This narrative is a journey of both interactivity and consequences – production alters the constituents in the soil with the soil being an agentic product (see Chapters 1 and 4) causing poor drainage, increased salt and the creation of a 'river' of waste water killing fish and birds. This example demonstrates that human and non-human interactions create actant risks shaping this riskscape.

Individualisation and risks

Relational definitions of risk shape riskscapes, creating uneven and unequal distribution of risks. Fundamental to revealing the operation and definitions of unequal risks is an examination of discourses of individualisation associated with land ownership which privilege agriculture as a way of life. Risk is revealed in these discourses as a risk to water allocation due to drought threatening farm business and livelihood. As Chapter 4 argued, frontier imaginaries shape agricultural development in the USA and Australia, reinforcing a discourse of individualisation embedded in settler discourses that underscore the ownership and controlling of nature for economic productivity. Individualisation, as expressed and experienced by irrigators, is a particular mode of subjectivation (Foucault, 2008). As Foucault (2008, p. 272) explains, individualisation as a subject position is based on individual choices, the pursuit of individual interests and the maximisation of profit. In irrigation communities water is the life force of production and therefore critical in maximising profit. Ownership of agricultural land is discursively understood synonymously with ownership of water. Indeed, irrigators understood their access to water as an economic and social 'right'.

In the Riverland the 'right' to individualised water access for irrigation became pronounced with newly transformed trade water rights, enabling the trading of water without recourse to the collective body of irrigators through the RIT (Horne, 2013). The freeing up of the market in 2007 under the Australian Competition and Consumer Commission (ACCC) allowed irrigators to trade water 'without the need for approval of an irrigation infrastructure operator' (Horne, 2013, p. 530). Internationally, scholars have noted tensions about water ownership and contestation related to changes to mechanisms for purchasing water (Bjornlund et al., 2010; Horne, 2013; Susskind, 2013; Tortajada, 2010). For irrigators in this study, tensions were aggravated between the needs of the individual and the RIT's remit, especially as water environments became increasingly stable with the breaking of the drought. Therefore, as uncertainty decreased, trust and the notion of the 'collective' also decreased. Irrigators explained:

> I reckon it would be nice if we could buy our own water. CIT [the other water trust in the district] do it and I reckon we are lacking because we can't.

> We kept all our licensing and it's our right to decide what happens with it. I don't think that RIT should come along and say 'you're more efficient now and so we can afford to take another thirty, forty per cent off you'. I think we should be allowed to decide the future for our own water in that sense – it is our license.

Irrigators were more focused on the individualisation of profit in times of abundant water flows rather than previous attitudes of collectivity during times of drought. Indeed, Riverland irrigators reconstructed their knowledge about water and its place in the market with increased water flows and returned to neo-liberal practices and forms of subjectivation. For irrigators, ultimately trust was contingent on the political economy and the conditions that gave rise to profit or loss. In times of financial stress, limited water flows and changing government policy, the irrigator requires the power of regulatory bodies to act in a collective fashion; however, when water flows increase and the threat of government reducing water allocations subsides, there is a return to individualisation (see Chapter 6).

In California the concept of individualisation is deeply embedded in relation to land and water ownership. As argued in Chapter 2, unlike Australian water laws, Californian laws do not refer to water allocation but water *rights*, thereby entrenching ideologies of individualised ownership of water. As Fitchen (1987, p. 7) argues 'by custom in the United States, ground water use is treated as a property right similar to mineral extraction rights'. Riparian doctrines enforce an ownership of the *right* to a percentage of the flow. Water rights under the appropriation water doctrine (see Chapter 2), the most common water doctrine in the USA, are based on where agricultural land is situated along the river flow and allows for the right to divert and use water based on the notion of 'first in time, first in right' (Tisdell, 2003, p. 405). Discourses of individualisation are embedded in US water legislation which are shaped by a series of *individual rights to water* related to ownership, property and temporal land purchase. Individualism is embedded in history, laws, and constitutional rights and in contestations about change to legislation. Underpinning all of these spheres are institutionally embedded ideologies of individualisaton.

The complexity of unchanging water laws in California promotes individualised and unequal ownership of water (see Chapter 2). California's riparian and appropriation water rights enable approximately 4,000 companies and farmers to use unmonitored water access without payment. For example, an irrigator and water trust manager explained why unlimited access to water was imperative for growers:

> Without water we can't farm ... like the almond trees I was talking about. We are basically a desert but we have the ability to apply water at the correct time and we have been very successful in expanding the demand for almonds. In fact, there are a lot of new almond tree plantings and orchards.

The growing of almonds is water intensive, requiring year round watering, and has been a recently introduced initiative in both sites. Almonds were introduced to compensate for low commodity prices for other produce – cotton in California and wine grapes in South Australia. Another participant who was involved in water board management explained the anguish that may come from conceptualising water as individually owned and reported:

> One man took his turn before another on the ditch water and an upset farmer killed his neighour – I mean it's amazing how people get upset over their water. I mean ownership is literal.

This tragic and extreme response illustrates the centrality of emotion associated with riskscapes where 'moral emotions, their place in social relations ... [have] potential for both function and dysfunction' (Skorupski, 2010, p. 158).

As the Californian drought worsens, tensions and conflicts around 'water rights' escalate around constructions of water as a public good or private right. The public good perspective focuses on water as a 'flow essential to life and ecosystem health; nonsubstitutable and tightly bound to communities' whilst understanding water as a private right commodifies water and places it in the realm of economics and the market (Bakker, 2007, p. 441). Bakker (2007, p. 440) has argued that a public/private binary of water rights tends to 'recognize only two unequally satisfactory options – state or market control: twinned corporatist models from which communities are equally excluded'. This binary of water rights evident in the complexity of water law in California has resulted in legal disputes between irrigators and between irrigators and other corporate bodies and the state. A number of participants referred to these lengthy and costly legal disputes over water access. A participant explained:

> conflicting water rights, who has the right to what there is always grey areas, and that's why they go to battle it out in law.

As Fitchen (1987, p. 7) suggests, 'in the legal system the collective nature of groundwater is not at all clearly established. In fact, US groundwater law is in flux and subject to differing court interpretations'. The question of 'reasonable requirements' in relation to irrigator's access to water under riparian doctrine has been at the centre of conflicts, given the ambiguity of the concept of 'reasonable' (Tisdell, 2003). While water laws provide fertile ground for litigation, a binary thinking about water rights inadequately addresses how water is used and controlled, as state intervention in water conservation occurs particularly during times of drought despite the privatisation of water (Kallis et al., 2010).

Risk and regulation

As we have argued, a critical dynamic in shaping riskscapes are state/corporate relations. Central to this social dynamic are the ways in which risks are made governable and negotiated between regulatory bodies and irrigators. In Foucauldian terms, the actions of those organisations constituted as an object, here the state and federal governments responsible for policy development and legislation, were understood by irrigators to exacerbate their vulnerabilities. There was significant discussion in relation to the political aspects of water management raised by all participants. Whether at the state or federal level, government interests were consistently identified as not in line with those of Riverland and Californian irrigators. These attitudes resembled the contested stakeholder domains in which water operates internationally (see Tortajada, 2010).

In the Riverland, speaking specifically about the local horticulturalists' interaction with the government, one irrigator suggested: 'I think they put their trust in the government or the leaders to come good. I don't really think that's been repaid lately and I think we're going to see a change in direction', referring to the shifting sense of trust the community had held thus far. Continuing, the irrigator highlighted the depth of mistrust in the government: 'politically, they don't care. I'm sure if we just disappeared, they wouldn't care, because they haven't shown anything to say that they do.'

There was a similar, if not more ardent tone, of distrust of the state in California, with an irrigator suggesting the drought was 'government induced due to new regulations on reclamation on the Delta'. Further, in the USA copious articles have appeared in the media about legal conflicts between irrigators and the state. An article appearing in the *Los Angeles Times* summarises the inherent individualised response to water by irrigators and the expanse between individual and collective ownership of water evident in the following quotation:

> 'The state … is coming in trying to regulate people who cannot be regulated for the benefit of people who don't want to be regulated,' said attorney — , who filed one of the lawsuits on behalf of the — Irrigation District.
>
> (Boxall, 2014)

In recent times, new bills have been brought before the Senate to regulate groundwater locally, thereby reducing state regulation (see Chapters 2 and 6). However, despite apprehension of state involvement in US regulation, in both sites discourses of individualisation and risk obscure state intervention in supporting agriculture, through subsidies in the USA and drought relief in Australia. In Australia in 2015 there was a suite of drought relief programs and loans to the value of AU$333 million to assist farm businesses, farm families and agricultural communities to manage and recover from drought (Department of Agriculture, 2015). The US federal government pays approximately $30 billion in subsidies to farmers including $851 million in disaster subsidies. In 2015 Fresno irrigators received $183 million federal funding and $678 million state funding (*Economist*, 2014).

This rendering of government action as objectionable was further evidenced through the discourse of 'us' and 'them' used by irrigators to discuss government policies, which they suggested showed a lack of understanding of the local contexts in which the policies were enacted. For many, there was a loss of local knowledges and expertise associated with government restructuring, as governments are distanced, both politically and geographically, from irrigation areas. Riverland growers reported:

> they don't live in the region, they don't know, they've got no social interaction so it's not the same [though] it might look good on a balance sheet.

> it's even more evident today that there is a lack of understanding by the people who run our country, the people who make decisions, there is a lack of understanding; one, how hard we worked, and sometimes for little reward, but the policies that they put in place and how hard they make it for Australian growers … we just cannot win.

Similarly, Californian irrigators explained:

the paper on the health of fish is more important for the legislature than what the farmers do with the water, because the farmers will always adapt and understand what they do.

This claim that local knowledges were dismissed may stem from a reaction to policy change where divergent and other knowledges entered the policy field, such as environmental scientists and urban community members threatening local rural knowledge (Gill, 2011; Horne, 2013). Also of particular concern to irrigators was a lack of recognition of their role as stewards of the land who operate efficiently. A Riverland participant commented:

> We are head and shoulders the number one region in terms of ... value per hectare ... we've become really efficient. So if you're going to make cuts why would you cut an area that's already got the infrastructure in place, already got the community functioning reasonably well?

> There is a complete lack of regard for people on the land, the food providers of this country ... the thing that government doesn't understand [is] the quality of the growers ... if you really understood the quality of the grower that you have, you would be putting policy out there that would preserve and encourage these people.

There is a body of international research which highlights the significance of such 'local knowledges' in relation to regulatory trust, suggesting that the interpersonal relationships embedded within a system play a vital role in facilitating trust, particularly in those complex situations where levels of uncertainty are greater (e.g. Hedgecoe, 2012; Tortajada, 2010). However, irrigators felt their expertise and knowledges were not respected, which was particularly dissonant given that, according to Foucault's (2008) conceptualisation of governable risk and biopolitical power, the individual must operate autonomously. Instead, irrigators reported that predominantly outside knowledges were understood to have more political power, both at the individual and state and federal levels.

Both sites compared their access to water and political clout in relation to other states. A Riverland participant suggested that due to South Australia's smaller population compared to other states and its geographical positioning in the MDB, its capacity to influence government policy in terms of water allocations was significantly less than other states, arguing:

> There has to be national control though ...What sort of a government have we got when they can't sort out a river system for everybody, you know? Just because we're in South Australia at the bottom end, that's ridiculous, it should be the same for everybody.
>
> (Irrigator, Renmark)

How do you allocate groundwater amongst all the users – one area is causing excessive withdrawal out of another area ... to set basin management objectives where you reach a certain elevation of water and everybody can only share down to those levels ... this would make sense.

(Irrigator, Central California)

This frustration with the perceived disregard for the local context and the resulting lack of trust in the regulatory bodies involved suggests that effective trust is only established through an acknowledgement of the situated knowledges held by local stakeholders (Bratspies, 2009; Hedgecoe, 2012; Möllering, 2006). As Luhmann (1998) suggests, because actors within the system cannot fully examine nor comprehend the system (because of the very fact that they are acting within it), instead they must rely upon the performance of the experts within the organisation to 'prove' that the system is working. In this way, it is possible the RIT may come under greater scrutiny and further issues of trust may appear if the experts themselves are unable to adequately advocate for the community in negotiations with state and federal governments. However, whilst irrigators distrusted the multiple levels of government as these were understood as separate from, and often in conflict with the local, in contrast the RIT's presence was significantly embedded in the local context and therefore a subject with whom trust could be established.

Conclusion

The concept of riskscapes provides a lens through which to examine how risks are revealed, given meaning, and lived through the body and come into being within and across communities and states. Water as a fundamental element of riskscape brings forth water/landscape as porous, open to multiplicity of knowledges, imaginaries, practices, policies, emotions and corporeal transformations. In this way the concept of risk becomes a phenomenon that is both variegated and unequally dispersed.

This chapter demonstrated that risk in irrigation communities manifests relationally, that is, risks are defined in relation to other regulating or advocacy bodies like the RIT or in relation to competing knowledges, discourse and capital as is especially the case in California. The theoretical lesson from this examination is that culture, nature and capital come together in unique ways spatially to not only reveal risk but to shape it and create uneven risks amongst subjects sharing the same spaces. It is these 'volatile configurations of the social and material' (Whatmore, 2003, p. 166) – and in this case it is water as materiality and the material economic conditions – that shape water access and quality, impinging on environmental and human well-being.

Embedded in relational definitions of risk are multiple and interconnecting discourses of individualisation. Discourses frame water as an individual right tied to ownership of property rather than a public good or an environmental concern, which then establishes a discursive frame that constitutes drought as risk to water allocation for irrigation and other corporate enterprises. Alongside these individualistic discourses sit settler or frontier imaginaries that reinforce an individualised relationship to water and land. Frontier imaginaries reproduce ideologies and practices about land and waterscapes, that is, that land/waterscapes are to be controlled, developed and made economically productive. In this way, through frontier imaginaries the economic needs of some over others become privileged. These multiple and intersecting discourses hold immense political power.

We have argued that discourses of individualisation shape riskscapes and these discursive frames are critical in how the politics of water allocation is played out in relation to irrigator–state–corporate relations. Common to both the Riverland and Central California, governments are perceived as in opposition to the 'rights' of irrigators' access to water. Irrigators in the Riverland largely contest government policies to alter water management and use through the RIT. The RIT is constructed by irrigators as a collective and knowing body in whom they place trust to manage risk – the risk being that government may not provide what irrigators deem as adequate water allocation. Hence, while irrigators may adopt the prescribed role of autonomous entrepreneur, they have need of organisations like RIT to foster collectivity in the community and to contest and shape government policies about water allocation. However, with the easing of drought, relationships between the RIT and their irrigator members shift, requiring the RIT to navigate this changed relationship in a manner that avoids reducing the irrigator's sense of autonomy and individuality (see Chapter 6).

Trust and distrust were fundamental conditions in contested relations between states and irrigators. In Central California these contested domains of distrust, lack of clarity in legislation around water access and individualised ideologies about the right to water often provide the conditions for litigious activity, especially for wealthy irrigators. Distrust of the state was an embodied reaction shaping the dimensions and extensiveness of perceived risk. Risk for irrigators was further exacerbated by a perception that rural knowledges or farming knowledges were secondary to environmental or scientific knowledges and secondary to urban perceptions of water and environment.

This chapter has demonstrated that riskscapes are shaped at the local level by a combination of factors: multiple knowledges; the power of capital to influence policy; the pressure irrigators as a collective can bring to bear on local regulatory bodies either within communities or states to shape water allocations; and conversely, the lack of power held by members of the community to shape and influence policy. Riskscapes are variegated and materially uneven. First, they are uneven through the corporeal, in relation to health and well-being and emotionally through feelings of powerlessness, power, anger or anguish. Second, riskscapes are uneven through differential material access to water shaped by access to finance. Risk definition is more than competing knowledges and ideologies, as capital is a crucial factor in shaping risk and waterscapes. It is now timely for further analyses of the interstices of the social, culture, nature and the economic (Castree, 2003) enabling a critical conceptualisation of multiple dimensions of materiality to include water, the body, economic power and living conditions.

References

Adam, B. and Van Loon, J., 2000. Introduction: repositioning risk; the challenge for social theory. In: B. Adam, U. Beck and J. Van Loon, eds, *The risk society and beyond: critical issues for social theory*. London: Sage, pp. 2–30.

Bachmann, R. and Zaheer, A., 2006. *Handbook of trust research*. Cheltenham: Edward Elgar.

Bakker, K., 2003. *An uncooperative commodity: privatizing water in England and Wales*. Oxford: Oxford University Press.

Bakker, K., 2007. The 'commons' versus the 'commodity': alter-globalization, anti-privatization and the human right to water in the global South. *Antipode*, 39(3), pp. 430–455.

Balazs, C.L., Morello-Frosch, R., Hubbard, A. and Ray, I., 2011. Social disparities in nitrate contaminated drinking water in the San Joaquin Valley. *Environmental Health Perspectives*, 119(9), pp. 1272–1278.

Balazs, C.L. and Ray, I., 2014. The drinking water disparities framework: on the origins and persistence of inequities in exposure. *American Journal of Public Health*, 104(4), pp. 603–611.

Barclay, L.J., Skarlicki, D.P. and Pugh, S.D., 2005. Exploring the role of emotions in injustice perceptions and retaliation. *Journal of Applied Psychology*, 90(4), pp. 629–643.

Beck, D., 1996. Risk society and the provident state. In: S. Lash, B. Szerszynski and B. Wynne, eds, *Risk, environment and modernity: towards a new ecology*. London: Sage, pp. 27–43.

Beck, G. and Kropp, C., 2011. Infrastructures of risk: a mapping approach towards controversies on risks. *Journal of Risk Research*, 14(1), pp. 1–16.

Beck, U., 1992. *Risk society: towards a new modernity*. London: Sage.

Bjornlund, H., Wheeler, S. and Cheeseman, J., 2010. Irrigators, water trading, the environment and debt: buying water entitlements for the environment. In: D. Connell and R. Grafton, eds, *Basin futures: water reform in the Murray-Darling Basin*. Canberra, ACT: Australian National University Press, pp. 291–302.

Boxall, B., 2014. Lawsuits over California water rights are a fight a century in the making. *Los Angeles Times*. Online. Available at: www.latimes.com/local/california/la-me-water-rights-legal-20150629–story.html (Accessed 14 August 2015).

Bratspies, R.M., 2009. Regulatory trust. *Arizona Law Review*, 51, pp. 575–631.

Braun, B. and Castree, N., 1998. *Remaking reality: nature at the millenium*. London: Routledge.

Bryant, L. and Garnham, B., 2013. Beyond discourses of drought: the micro-politics of the wine industry and farmer distress. *Journal of Rural Studies*, 32, pp. 1–9.

Bryant, L. and Garnham, B., 2014. Economies, ethics and emotions: farmer distress within a moral economy of agribusiness. *Journal of Rural Studies*, 34, pp. 304–312.

Bryant, L. and George, J., 2016. Examining uncertainty and trust among irrigators and regulatory bodies in the Murray-Darling basin. *International Journal of Water Resources Development*, 32(1), pp. 102–115.

Bunton, R. and Petersen, A., eds, 1997. *Foucault, health and medicine*. London: Routledge.

Candlin, C.N. and Crichton, J., eds, 2013. *Discourses of trust*. Basingstoke: Palgrave Macmillan.

Carmin, J. and Agyeman, J., eds, 2011. *Environmental inequalities beyond borders: local perspectives on global injustices*. Cambridge, MA: MIT Press.

Castree, N., 2003. Commodifying what nature? *Progress in human geography*, 27(3), pp. 273–297.

Cook, K.S., ed., 2003. *Trust in society*. Volume II in the Russell Sage Foundation series on trust. New York: Russell Sage Foundation.

Dalby, S., 2007. Ecology, security, and change in the anthropocene. *Brown Journal of World Affairs*, 14(2), p. 155.

Dean, M., 1999. *Governmentality: power and rule in modern society*. London: Sage.

Department of Agriculture, 2015. Supporting farmers and rural communities in drought. Press release, 27 May. Available at: www.agriculture.gov.au/SiteCollectionDocuments/ag-food/drought/assistance-measures/supporting-farmers-rural-communities-in-drought.pdf (Accessed 31 May 2015).

Elliott, A., 2002. Beck's sociology of risk: a critical assessment. *Sociology*, 36, pp. 293–315.

Fitchen, J.M., 1987. Cultural aspects of environmental problems: individualism and chemical contamination of groundwater. *Science, Technology and Human Values*, 12(2), pp. 1–12.

Foucault, M., 1998 [1976]. *The history of sexuality. Volume 1: the will to knowledge*. London: Sage.

Foucault, M., 2008. *The birth of biopolitics: lectures at the collège de France, 1978–1979*. G. Burchell, trans. New York: Picador.

Fukuyama, F., 1995. *Trust: the social virtues and the creation of prosperity*. New York: Free Press.

Giddens, A., 1990. *Consequences of modernity*. Cambridge: Polity Press.

Gill, F., 2011. Responsible agents: responsibility and the changing relationship between farmers and the state. *Rural Society*, 20(2), pp. 128–141.

Haraway, D., 1988. Situated knowledges: the science question in feminism and the privilege of partial perspective. *Feminist studies*, 14(3), pp. 575–599.

Hedgecoe, A.M., 2012. Trust and regulatory organisations: the role of local knowledge and facework in research ethics review. *Social Studies of Science*, 42, pp. 662–683.

Higgins, V., 2001. Calculating climate: advanced liberalism and the governing of risk in Australian drought policy. *Journal of Sociology*, 37(3), pp. 299–316.

Horne, J., 2013. Economic approaches to water management in Australia. *International Journal of Water Resources Development*, 29, pp. 526–543.

Kallis, G., Ray, I., Fulton, J. and McMahon, J.E., 2010. Public versus private: does it matter for water conservation? Insights from California. *Environmental management*, 45(1), pp. 177–191.

Lash, S., 2000. Risk culture. In: Adam, B., Beck, U. and Van Loon, J., eds, *The risk society and beyond: critical issues for social theory*. London: Sage, pp. 47–62.

Latour, B., 1999. On recalling ANT. In: J. Law and J. Hassard, eds, *Actor network theory and after*. Oxford and Malden, MA: Wiley, pp. 15–25.

Lewicki, R.J. and Bunker, B.B., 1996. Developing and maintaining trust in work relationships. In: R. Kramer and T.R. Tyler, eds, *Trust in organizations: frontiers of theory and reach*. London: Sage, pp. 114–139.

Lewis, J.D. and Weigart, A.J., 2012. The social dynamics of trust: theoretical and empirical research, 1985–2012. *Social Forces*, 91, pp. 25–31.

London, J., Huang, G. and Zagofsky, T., 2011. Land of risk/land of opportunity: cumulative environmental vulnerability in California's San Joaquin valley. Davis: University of California–Davis Center for Regional Change.

Luhmann, N., 1998. *Observations on modernity*. Stanford, CA: Stanford University Press.

Lupton, D., 1992. Discourse analysis: A new methodology for understanding the ideologies of health and illness. *Australian Journal of Public Health*, 16(2), pp. 145–150.

Maseele, P. , 2015. Risk conflicts, critical discourse analysis, and media discourses on GM crops and food. *Journalism*, 16, pp. 278–297.

Möllering, G., 2006. Trust, institutions, agency: towards a neo-institutional theory of trust. In: R. Bachmann and A. Zaheer, eds, *Handbook of trust research*. Cheltenham: Edward Elgar, pp. 355–376.

Morello-Frosch, R., Pastor, M. and Sadd, J., 2001. Environmental justice and Southern California's 'riskscape': the distribution of air toxics exposures and health risks among diverse communities. *Urban Affairs Review*, 36(4), pp. 551–578.

Müller-Mahn, D., ed., 2012. *The spatial dimension of risk: how geography shapes the emergence of riskscapes*. London: Routledge.

Neisser, F. M., 2014. 'Riskscapes' and risk management: review and synthesis of an actor-network theory approach. *Risk Management*, 16(2), pp. 88–120.

November, V., 2008. Spatiality of risk. *Environment and Planning A*, 40, pp. 1523–1527.

Oels, A., 2005. Rendering climate change governable: from biopower to advanced liberal government? *Journal of Environment Policy and Planning*, 7, pp. 185–207.

Pautz, M.C., 2009. Trust between regulators and the regulated: a case study of environmental inspectors and facility personnel in Virginia. *Politics and Policy*, 37, pp. 1047–1072.

Price, L. and Evans, N., 2009. From stress to distress: conceptualizing the British family farming patriarchal way of life. *Journal of Rural Studies*, 25(1), pp. 1–11.

Rosa, E., Renn, O. and McCright, A., 2013. *The risk society revisited: social theory and governance*. Philadelphia, PA: Temple University Press.

Schlosberg, D., 2013. Theorising environmental justice: the expanding sphere of a discourse. *Environmental Politics*, 22(1), pp. 37–55.

Skorupski, J., 2010. *The domain of reasons*. Oxford: Oxford University Press.

Susskind, L., 2013. Water and democracy: new roles for civil society in water governance. *International Journal of Water Resources Development*, 29, pp. 666–677.

Sze, J. and London, J.K., 2008. Environmental justice at the crossroads. *Sociology Compass*, 2(4), pp. 1331–1354.

Szerszynski, B., 1999. Risk and trust: the performative dimension. *Environmental Values*, 8(2), pp. 239–252.

Tisdell, J.G., 2003. Equity and social justice in water doctrines. *Social Justice Research*, 16(4), pp. 401–415.

The Economist, 2014. The drying of the West: drought is forcing westerners to consider wasting less water. 22 February.

Tortajada, C., 2010. Water governance: some critical issues. *International Journal of Water Resources Development*, 26, pp. 297–307.

Walker, G., 2009. Beyond distribution and proximity: exploring the multiple spatialities of environmental justice. *Antipode*, 41(4), pp. 614–636.

Whatmore, S., 2003. Generating materials. In: M. Pryke, G. Rose and S. Whatmore, eds, *Using social theory: thinking through research*. London: Sage, pp. 89–104.

6 Community futures

Introduction

Discourses of risk, rights, unity, individualism, conservation and loss are articulated and enacted in relation to the absence of water or, more aptly, what may be considered *adequate* water during conditions of drought. Inevitably, irrigator responses to drought and water allocations are situated within the larger, yet generally unstated, context of temporality; the progression of time through the past, present and future of drought. Explored extensively during the spatial turn of the 1980s and 1990s (e.g. Gregory and Urry, 1985; Jameson, 1991; Lefebvre, 1991; Soja, 1989), the importance of understanding temporality as an aspect of landscapes and 'waterscapes' is significant. According to Massey (1992, p. 77), space and time are 'inextricably interwoven' as space may be understood as a *social* product and *society* as a spatial product, which are each constructed within a mutual relationship that relies upon history.

Following Massey, we argue that the temporality of irrigation communities is indeed politicised, as shifting environmental concerns, economic influences and stakeholders in water governance challenge expectations about community futures. The concept of temporality is used to examine how irrigators' understandings of community futures are challenged by the occurrence of drought. We explore how the politics of the irrigation space and its relationship to time during drought become apparent as irrigators begin to rehearse a different form of temporality in which the past, present and future are collapsed to establish a greater sense of control. The narratives of Australian and US irrigators show that previous seasons' water allocations are made to service the present, and the present is made to service the future, via increasing demands for control through stipulated water allocations. Control is executed through reflexive actions that culminate in collective advocacy and resistance, in efforts to assert water as an individualised right.

We also examine what happens as communities emerge from drought, focusing specifically on the Riverland, to understand how future imaginings are made possible as 'normality' is restored. During drought, irrigators are primarily concerned with the present and future imaginings appear limited.

However, when drought breaks, and the future does *become* the present, how might the focus on the sustainability of community futures shift? Attempts to shore up against future drought appear absent, as new ideas like tourism are expounded as a potential way forward for sustaining community futures. Community futures remain unpredictable but we argue that like the present, they take shape through an intersecting of past, present and future, thereby influencing the water practices of states, as well as the biographies and practices of irrigators.

Critical temporalities and communities

Time is critical to constituting communities and 'questions about the speed, pace and directionality of time are crucial to ... explaining communal futures and pasts' (Bastian, 2014, p. 138). Grosz (1999, p. 1) reminds us that 'time is more intangible than any other "thing", less able to be grasped, conceptually or physically'. Taking on board the ephemeral nature of time, in this chapter we understand transrural places as becoming and hence the futurity of the communities in question will unfold in both unexpected and expected ways. A becoming of community is informed by the interstices of time and space, which are not easily disengaged from each other. The time–space dynamic suggests time and space traverse to unfold multiple experiences (Massey, 1991) allowing for the 'simultaneous existence of different temporalities in space' (Lombard, 2013, p. 815), as well as the 'reciprocal influence of time on space' (Crang and Travlou, 2001, p. 175).

Social geographers provide multiple examples of space-time shaping place, in particular in the context of cities (e.g. Crang and Travlou, 2001; Lombard, 2013; Till, 2012). For example, Lombard (2013) discusses how residents become empowered and enact social change through turning to the past to constitute imagined futures. This connection of past, present and future imaginings enables an unsettling of present spatialities (Lombard, 2013, p. 823). Similarly, Crang and Travlou's (2001) focus on Athens shows that 'Athens [with its varied historic buildings] forms an absent origin, but that the past remains and becomes the present' with these moments in time 'crossing, folding and piercing' each other (2001, p. 162). Both these examples demonstrate that communities are neither fixed nor stable but are each in a process of becoming – intertwining present, past and future. As Lombard suggests (2013, p. 815), 'places can be understood as always becoming, with complex multiple temporalities underlying their dynamic progress'.

Indeed, in order to examine possible community futures, or more accurately to understand narratives that are brought into being to frame potential futures, it is important to understand the ways the 'past-present-future' are configured. Scholars commonly theorise the past as 'selectively constructed around a particular group's narrative and memories' (Bastian, 2014, p. 148) (see Chapter 3). The present may be conceived 'as an absence; by what it is *not* than what it *is*' (Crang and Travlou, 2001, p. 168, citing Bergson, 1991, p. 149, original emphasis in Crang and Travlou, 2001). The present then, rather than being a series of moments in time, is instead a 'becoming that erases itself' (Crang and Travelou, 2001, p. 168). Memories and narratives are organised around the present and future and therefore the present brings the past into focus, 'contracting it into the future and dilating into the past' (Crang and Travlou, 2001, p. 169). The unfolding and folding of the past-present-future is articulated by Deleuze (1988, p. 55, emphasis in original):

> the present is not; rather it is pure becoming, always outside itself. It is not, but it acts. Its proper element is not being but the active or useful. The past, on the other hand, has ceased to act or be useful. But it has not ceased to be. Useless, inactive, impassive it IS, in the full sense of the word.

The past works its way toward the present and the future. The future is linked to desires and hopes and as such, has the capacity to disturb the present (Lombard, 2013). Grosz (2005) draws our attention to the unpredictability of the future and its attendant uncertainties, which can cause anxieties at multiple scales – for individuals, communities and societies. In relation to questions about water and climate change, the future is often constituted as far reaching and apocalyptic (Williams and Booth, 2013, p. 26). This positioning of climate change as a future threat can mean that we are unable to 'conceptualize time beyond the periodic frame of our own lifetimes, or even a generation, and [are unable] to imagine distant futures in which the climate might be altered' (Brace and Geoghegan, 2010, p. 292).

If the past, present and future are narrated in particular ways that mobilise certain political positions then multiple and different positions may not always be heard or given the same space within histories (see Chapter 4). Consequently, like their pasts and their present, the articulation of possible community futures is also political. As Taylor aptly states (2013, p. 829), inequalities are 'Distinctions [that] occur in time and place, meaning some cannot easily "move forward" or travel to a "new" future place …' Inequalities mean that some futures are less evoked than others 'in past-present-future encounters' and 'certain places and certain people are meant to "become" or arrive in place' (Taylor, 2013, p. 830). Critical temporalities point to social inequalities in constituting hegemonic meanings about community and in shaping future imaginaries. Critical temporality brings to light that any future imaginary will consist of multiple envisionings and be a contested terrain. However, as Grosz (1999, pp. 6–7) would argue, this chapter is not about 'predicting what will happen, nor is it an exercise in futurology … rather it explores the various ontological, epistemological, political and social implications of considering time in terms of supervalence of the future'.

The rehearsal of history as a touchstone for the present

Historical connections to the land, as inscribed in legislation and in past practices and knowledges, shape the contours of irrigation communities into the present and future. As Chapter 2 indicated, nineteenth-century water allocation laws in California allow water rights to irrigators who originally staked claims on rivers and streams. Under this historical regime, amounts of water used are reported by agricultural producers and corporations to the state. Thus, in Central California water legislation is a platform for contemporary and future accessibility to water. At the forefront of all US participant narratives was the recitation of the history of water rights development. Participants outlined the introduction of legislation, detailing which districts and irrigators benefit from greater water allocations. Participants explained that whilst legislative provisions set the parameters for how water is allocated, water allocation becomes more complex in relation to extracting ground water. An irrigator explained that despite drought, irrigators could still 'freely' access ground water:

> You can depend on the rain, but we only get about five inches of rain a year, and of course, we're in the middle of a drought ... You can mine it from the ground, which our district does to a degree. And here in California, at least in our area, we don't have any laws yet governing the extraction of groundwater, so we're completely free to do that.
> (Irrigation District director)

Referring to 'free' access to ground water reinforces an assumed right to water that is located on their landholding. In this way, land and water are inextricably linked to ownership of property in the memories of these participants. An individual rights-based discourse regarding ownership of land and water is then translated into the present in defending and arguing for contemporary water allocations. An irrigator explained:

> there's no groundwater laws ... although some counties have said 'you can pump water but you can't sell pumped water out of the county' as opposed to surface water ... farmers want to be free as business people to sell their water if they want.

The word 'free' appears again, suggesting that irrigators are entrepreneurs who have the right to buy and sell 'their water'. These free actions in using and accessing water have often resulted in inaccurate reporting of the amounts of water being used, creating difficulties for the state to measure water availability and therefore appropriately govern.

Whilst irrigators in Central California argue for 'free' access to ground water, Governor Brown has introduced restrictions on the use of ground water (Green, 2014). The acknowledgement in law of both ground and surface water is a first in Californian water history. The 2014 Groundwater Regulation Act does not allow the state to ban pumping but puts in place local regulatory bodies to monitor and manage ground and surface water (Green, 2014). As Green (2014, p. 429) states:

> The Act requires groundwater management practices to be 'sustainable' ... and to satisfy this new requirement, a local management agency's plan must include an approximate sustainable yield for the basin it oversees.

The purpose of the Act is to increase water supply and limit environmental damage. However, given the ambiguity of the term 'sustainability' and an absence of 'enforcement ability, the state would be forced to return to the sluggish court system' to attempt to enforce regulatory requirements (Green, 2014, p. 433).

Irrigators have continued to protest that any changes to groundwater rights must be adjudicated through the judicial system. Indeed, the Californian Farm Bureau Federation has been vocal in disputing these legislative changes, arguing that lawsuits will follow. Media reports illustrate that those critical of the legislation frame their counter-position on the basis of democratic rights: 'With the stroke of a pen, the governor changed over 100 years of water laws – without the people's input' (Miller, 2014).

Indeed, Jim Nielson, rancher and Republican state assemblyman, was also reported as stating 'This is not the democracy that California deserves' (Miller, 2014). Green (2014, p. 435) succinctly summarises the political stance of irrigators:

> opponents fear that little control will remain with the owners of the land overlying certain basins. Because of this possibility, local landowners who have enjoyed free reign over their water for decades would like to limit the state's intervention power to a narrowly applied and scarcely used backstop, exercised only when absolutely necessary.

Since the introduction of the legislation there have been curtailment notices issued to farmers requiring a cessation of any diverting of water from rivers and streams. As a consequence, litigation has been resorted to by several farmers from Central Valley, resulting in temporary restraining orders blocking the state from fining or using other punitive measures toward farmers who have continued to divert water for their own use.

Hydrologists have suggested that regulatory measures require more stringent changes as farmers from Central Valley have managed to block the state only a year on from the introduction of the legislation. In addition, it appears likely that ground and surface water will be managed locally by upstream irrigators and those who have 'free' access to groundwater, raising concerns about conflicts of interest in regulating and reporting water use (Green, 2014). Moreover, where similar laws have been passed in other states there has been little change to water practices. Thus, by drawing on the past, irrigators are contouring their present and their futures in agriculture and through successful court action continue to obtain unhindered access to groundwater. Policy makers, on the other hand, are also attempting to shape community futures by defending their proposed legislative changes.

In the Riverland, court action over water use is rare. Members of the Renmark community rehearsed their history in relation to their familial histories with the land, where inheritance of property and intergenerational farming practices inform the present and potential futures. Participants recall the multiple generations who have lived and worked on the land they now own. As one irrigator explained, 'there's been the advantage that kids could go on to follow in their family's footsteps, and their grandparents' footsteps with horticulture'.

For many, this personal citation of association between past and present generations was an important way of establishing their historical credentials as irrigators who have 'proven', through longevity and productivity, their right to water allocations. Moreover, it is not uncommon for farmers in many parts of the world to draw on family experiences in understanding themselves, their business and how to farm (Brandth and Haugen, 2000; Bryant, 1999). As Kuehne (2013, p. 203), an Australian researcher and farmer, has argued:

> I understand the farming environment because I have experienced it at a time and in a way that has left its mark ... the power of tradition meant that in some ways the choice to become a farmer was never consciously made – I was destined to be a farmer.

For some farmers, tradition through family association with farming is an important aspect in constituting identity (Brandth and Haugen, 2000; Bryant, 1999) and as such, this past narrative and understanding of self is called into the present to defend water rights and to defend possibilities for themselves and their successors to continue to farm into the future (see Chapter 3).

For Central Californian irrigators, their historical narrative tends to be drawn from the public sphere, based on legislative developments over time and historical conditions. As we have argued, disputes over ownership of water continue through litigious activities around water access (see

Chapter 2). Litigious action is understood as a taking back of what is 'rightfully theirs'. An irrigator explained:

> we've had water taken away and if agriculture is ever going to come back to anything to near what it was, well the water has to come back at a reasonable price and at the right time … this is a time rife with litigious activity.

This 'publicly' drawn narrative informs current actions and understandings of water and orientations for the future. We are suggesting that this narrative is public as, first, it is drawn from the public arena of recorded history and legislation, and second, it is rehearsed in public, that is, in the media and in the courts. The use of public narratives as a form of policy engagement has a temporal location, as this form of social action is a call to action in the present. Hence, it is a form of a resistance and a call to collectivity as the development and rehearsal of this narrative draws irrigators together (see following section). Nevertheless, this publicly inspired narrative is also deeply personal and folds into private histories and narratives of farming. The story of 'us' as Californian irrigators and 'our rights' to water is also a story of 'me', a Californian irrigator who owns water for productive purposes. While Renmark irrigators gave greater attention to family biographies, they also drew on public narratives embedded in frontier imaginaries of settlement to understand their present, as indicated in Chapters 3 and 4. As a consequence, there is not a simple public/private binary in the way histories are remembered and presented across the study sites. We reiterate that all irrigators mobilise the past to inform present and future water access but they mobilise the past in different ways, as discussed in the next section.

Shaping water policies, shaping futures

In both the Riverland and Central California, the policy arena becomes the theatre of water allocation politics, where irrigators attempt to shape futures. In the Riverland, efforts to act as a collective, a collective of irrigators through the water trust but also a growing collective inclusive of governing bodies beyond those with the remit for irrigation, is a primary means for crafting futures. Collectivity here is in anticipation of 'the common' or the common 'good' and thus 'political struggles can be identified as always-already configuring themselves through active enactments of … diverse subjectivities' who co-operate for the 'good' of the community (Dunst and Edwards, 2011, p. 5). In contrast, in Central California the policy domain becomes increasingly an arena of debate as new drought-based regulations become possibilities in this region. In both sites, forms of collectivity become a measure of resistance to non-agricultural voices and state and federal politics.

The Riverland community: futures and policy engagement

As argued in the previous chapter, Riverland irrigators turn to their water trust as a means of advocating for the interests of members in an attempt to secure their productive future. They rely on the Trust to shape policy in order to reduce uncertainty and attempt to 'know' the future in an effort to control potential threats to reduced water allocations. Threats are controlled by negotiating for water allocations, being alert to potential policy changes that may threaten the interests of irrigators and advocating for sound infrastructure for the delivery of water. Thus, through the Trust present activities become a conduit for future possibilities. By engaging the Trust to manage risk, subjects reflexively manage the individualisation of risk. In this way 'subjects are enlisted in the ethical government of their own embodied temporal orientation' (Binkley, 2009, p. 89). Binkley (2009, p. 89) has developed Beck's and Giddens' theorisation of risk (see Chapter 5) to incorporate a pre-reflexive dimension, that is, 'the part of the self upon which the reflexive self acts' whilst including their understanding of reflexivity as a cognitive, calculated, reflexive endeavour. The point being made by Binkley is that reflexivity includes at times an awareness and at other times an habituated response. In relation to irrigators, it is the awareness of risk which gives us an insight into their 'rationally derived temporal futures' (Binkley, 2009, p. 91). Irrigators were unable to individually manage risk as drought continued and policy debates became fraught, threatening further reduced water allocations. However, irrigators attempted to avert reduced allocations through collective action. For example:

> We as individuals can do very little, we need the organisation.

> being with a large group of people, you're not out on a limb on your own, if you've got any issues, you've got someone to turn to and someone to speak on your behalf.

As Chapter 5 demonstrated, uncertainty and powerlessness are reduced for irrigators when trust is operationalised through seeking collective action and advocacy from the Renmark Irrigation Trust. Feeling 'not on your own' suggests collectivity is a means to escape feelings of powerlessness but is also a powerful act of agency. There is an 'anticipatory regard for the future' (Binkley, 2009, p. 94), whereby collectivity is a strategy to mobilise against risk to protect futures.

Collectivity as a strategy grew as the momentum of threats increased. Irrigators believed South Australia required a voice to 'fight' the other states for their required water allocation. Collective action now involved the inclusion of competitors, that is, other irrigation trusts in the region and support from local governments and other stakeholder bodies to manage the possibilities that irrigators from other states located upstream would receive greater water allocations. At this point, South Australian irrigators began to redefine threats, as risks became heightened by inter-state rivalries over water access. As one irrigator commented:

> is it fair that New South Wales is getting 95 per cent and they don't have the water efficiencies that we've got and we're only getting 32 per cent? No, no fair ... they put us in a pretty uncompetitive position.

Another irrigator revealed his understanding of the political positioning of South Australia:

> South Australia's the poor relation ... in the long run we'll have less say about what happens and be the recipient of the decisions that are made largely outside of our control by upstream uses and the more popular states of Victoria, New South Wales and Queensland.

The understanding that other states have an 'unfair' advantage in relation to water allocation and are less 'efficient' than South Australia illustrates the political struggles for water access occurring across Australia. Here, as Bakker (2012, p. 616) argues, 'water ... defies jurisdictions, pits upstream against downstream users'. Multiple levels of governance of water, state by state, federally and at the local regional level creates complex geopolitics surrounding access. In this way, water becomes 'a boundary object ... allied with various forms of governance' (Bakker, 2012, p. 618). As a downstream user, South Australia receives water that is affected by upstream use (Quiggin, 2001). Indeed, the history of Australia is one coloured by state disputes in relation to claims to property rights of water from the Murray–Darling Basin (Quiggin, 2001). This history folds into the present to inform contemporary regional understandings of water access and questions of efficiency and fairness.

Central California futures and policy engagement

Like the Riverland, for Central California drought has meant the enforcement of new governmental policies and regulations. Indeed, in the USA and Australia drought has been the 'centrepiece of government policy' (Kiem and Austin, 2013, p. 1315) used to legitimise water reforms, allowing legislators to distance themselves from discourses associated with river health and ecological needs (Edwards, 2013, p. 1874). At present, 'climate change is being used to explain *future* water scarcity' (Edwards, 2013, p. 1882, emphasis in original) and mobilise increasing regulations aimed at increasing efficiency.

Many participants discussed how increasing levels of drought accompanied increasing regulation. For example, 'This year is going to be a very interesting

Community futures 121

year ... the policy process has been very active in the last few years' (water industry professional). As discussed earlier in this chapter, the communities of Central California responded to proposed and changing policy and water governance in multiple, and at times, conflicting ways (see Chapter 5). First, like the Riverland, there was evidence of resistance by irrigators. Across the landscapes of Fresno, irrigators had erected multiple signs condemning actions by Congress in relation to water allocations. Roadside signs blamed Congress for creating a 'dustbowl' and for reduced water allocations (Figures 6.1 and 6.2). These signs were hoisted on fences or staked into the dry earth

Figure 6.1 'Congress' flawed laws', Central California

122 *Community futures*

Figure 6.2 'Politicians created the water crisis', Central California

on a highway turnoff at the entrance of established agricultural properties. They were placed in a position to catch the eye of those travelling into or out of the district. Further, the signs were *situated* in landscape. Their material presence was located around grey, cracked earth and loose top soil, confronting the viewer with the barrenness of the landscape and the absence of water. Hence, the viewer is challenged with what is absent as well as present. In this space, the signage takes on meaning in context of the landscape which surrounds it. Signs and space act like an artefact to convey emotions that may not arise from the words printed on the signs alone (e.g. Tilley, 2006). In combination the signs and their placement bring forth an emotional and sensory impact on the viewer. They illicit emotions associated with loss, a loss of productive earth and a loss of a vibrant landscape. The placement of these signs produces feelings that are in contrast to growth and renewal, suggesting a downward spiral of inactivity and death of the landscape. The words on the signs work alongside what is absent and present in the landscape to portray a causal relationship between landscape and politics, one in which Congress is at fault.

Moreover, the impact of the signs is heightened and mediated by present knowledges, practices and experiences of drought for those living nearby. In particular, current irrigator knowledges and water practices associated with drought are inscribed on both signs, reinforcing a rights-based discourse in relation to water allocation. The message on the first sign suggests that changes to water allocations are unjust for irrigators and clearly articulates the power of irrigators to 'change Congress' if water allocations are reduced. The second sign reinterprets the drought as a created 'water crisis' which has occurred through state intervention.

Like the buildings of the Riverland Irrigation Trust, these photos become sites and sights of meaning established in place (see Chapter 4). However, these signs are not reminiscent of a past shaping a present, they are a present that challenges the future. They make resistance tangible and visible, demonstrating the 'need to remedy ... a "lack of a future"' (Binkley, 2009, p. 102). In this way, 'individuals reflect back on their own embodied temporal orientations, to feel compelled to expand their own future orientation' (Binkley, 2009, p. 102). The message of resistance is that the near future requires change and evidence of mobilisation and these signs show irrigator 'attempts to refigure ... encounters with space ... [and] time' (Rose and Tolia-Kelly, 2012, p. 1). Yet, to challenge the future these signs which represent a political position, or as Haraway (1988) would suggest, an embodied politics of envisioning, must be read in the way the creator intended. As argued in Chapter 4, relations of power shape what 'matter' matters and to whom, and in this way there are multiple possibilities and limitations in what and how one sees (Ahmed, 2004).

The second point about policy engagement and community future is associated with multiple ways of envisioning the future. As Chapter 5 demonstrated, lobbyists and environmentalists from Central California discussed differential water rights and access systems as a determinant of community futures. Hence, risk was also being reflexively calculated, showing the multiple and active ways threats were made known and the embodied work undertaken to reduce risk. In particular, there was a fear for the future in relation to unchanged agricultural practices. There were concerns about discrepancies in water costings due to the type of infrastructure delivering the water and concerns that the broader community, that is, the state, would be penalised through paying accumulated financial debt. Hence, there were understandings that agriculture was holding community futures hostage. For example:

> it disproportionally benefits certain people, developers, agribusiness, those are the primary beneficiaries of these big public water projects.
> (Journalist, Central California)

> they're going to saddle future generations of California … I think it's about 10 per cent to 15 per cent of our budget every year is bond repayment, billions of dollars that could be going to help people.
> (Lobbyist, Central California)

In Central California, there was fracture and tension within the community about water use and allocations as past and present water practices appear to collapse into future possibilities for communities. Poor living conditions for some are exacerbated and any change in water practice becomes unlikely given that the wealthy have a stronghold on policy development. As one journalist highlighted, 'The old money is like a rock, but the people on the fringes [are excluded]'. Similarly, as a water industry professional suggested, 'that's one of the big policy issues in California … the big running rough shod over everybody'. Californian water politics exemplifies Massey's (2005, p. 71) contention that land/waterscapes are socio-spatial relations occurring in 'the realm of the configuration of potentially dissonant (or concordant) narratives … that [bring] distinct temporalities into new configurations'. Consequently, making visible 'contested imaginaries' (Brace and Geoghegan, 2010, p. 296) enables an assessment of potential trajectories for communities' futures 'without being able to anticipate a destination' (Grosz, 1999, p. 19).

Riverland and Central California: water as personal product

Policy engagement and debate in both the Riverland and Central California was approached differently; however, each community understood that during times of drought, water was a 'product' that was owned by irrigators. This personal nature of understanding ownership of water spills into the public domain, bringing irrigators together as a collective or in the case of Central California, a group of wealthy producers, to fight the state and shape policy in their favour. Approaches to risk and drought show that past-present-futures interrupt and intersect to constitute personal biographies which themselves inform and are informed by water practices and policies. The agentic response to drought is reflexive work and 'what is being worked on is the embodied temporality of daily practice' (Binkley, 2009, p. 102) to create particular futures.

The breaking of drought and the return to cyclical understandings of time

The meanings and practices of water discussed so far have focused on drought. In the Riverland the drought broke during 2011. With the breaking of drought irrigators' responses to shaping policy collectivity simply stopped. As the immediate threat dissipated, and the crisis was averted, the situation was understood as a 'return to normal' water practices and perhaps a pre-reflexive practice of farming. Binkley (2009, p. 100), drawing on Bourdieu, discusses pre-reflexive practice and its impact on action, (un)certainty and time, arguing that through:

> embodied competence in the execution of practices, time literally flies by – unimpeded actions require little thought or reflection and life is lived on 'automatic pilot'. But when the practice of daily life is characterized by a lack of fit between habitus and field, where the felt promise or possibility of action emerges as increasingly uncertain in relation to the objective circumstances of action, agents view their own embodied expectations and their somatic orientations to the future outcomes of action as problematic; they are prone to a reflexive disposition in regard to the risks and futures of their own conduct.

Whilst threat and being at risk is not a condition of reflexivity or of actions that orient us toward futures, threat may enable an emergent reflexivity produced from a disjuncture. This disjuncture emerges, 'where the sense of mastery of playing the game is drawn into question, and where the utility of taken-for-granted knowledge in realizing desired outcomes enters a state of crisis' (Binkley, 2009, p. 100).

As a result, the past may take on a different framing, only *part* of a recurring timeline that is neither so enmeshed nor immediate in the consciousness of irrigators, and the present orientation becomes one which is limited in its engagement with water politics. For irrigators, there may be no real sense of urgency to understand 'what do we do next time' when drought recurs, limiting the perceived need for collectivity. As one Renmark irrigator explained:

> when things got really good, people sort of have moved away from each other, people don't need each other anymore so therefore that sense of community is not as strong as it was.

Although factors such as commodity prices, imported products and infrastructure upgrades continue to contribute to possible uncertainty for irrigators, the reduction in the immediacy of water needs means the temporality of the future is framed simply as a continuation of the present. Time becomes part of a recurring history, as one participant explained:

> When I came up here in '93 things were tough; things weren't good ... and then things got good and things got extra good – over the top basically and then the crash came.

Despite this focus on the present as an isolated point in time or as part of a recurring cycle that is without major moments of differentiation, what is interesting is that many irrigators convey an awareness of the possibility of drought, but this does not appear to necessitate action during times of adequate water flows. As irrigators explained:

> I guess I've got enough water up my sleeve and at the end of the day I'm not using it to put bread on the table ... I could probably ride it out.

And another irrigator similarly stated:

> I haven't got any major plans for future droughts but being in a trust we can't buy more but I believe it will be fine, as a whole you see it will work out and all it comes back to is that it will cost us a lot more money.

In these narratives, water easily meets the needs for productivity and livelihood and therefore being able 'to ride it out' if there is a reduction in water in the short term thereby reduces the threat to farming. Water is no longer on the agenda as a scarce resource. Instead, what was once the catastrophic crisis of drought appears to become part of a normalised narrative where danger exists only in the most extreme of cases. These narratives reinforce meanings of water as a taken for granted part of the land/waterscape. In the words of this irrigator, water is 'always going to be there':

> you'll have a three year drought, then you'll have a four or five year good period, and then you may have two seasons of wet season, and then it comes back to drought ... the water's always going to be there, unless you have a fifteen year drought.

Another irrigator affirmed:

> I think that water always finds its own ... in three years' time you'll see a very different landscape, but I'm sure you'll see a good landscape.

The turn in narratives from risk, disaster, and collapse of community to 'water always finds its own' suggesting there will always be water is a dramatic shift. In these scenarios, the present and the future will now take care of themselves and the idea that rain will come is an assumption associated with predictable cycles of nature. In this way, 'the past and the future only exist in relation to the present ... and the future projected from the present' (Gill, 2013, pp. 82–83). For farmers, temporality is straddled to make future decisions and though in Australia drought is recurrent, there is no incorporation of past experiences of drought into shaping present and future. The narratives imply a becoming of community where there will be little change to water practices and river health. In this way the future is linked to desires and hopes as Lombard (2013) suggests, but rather than hope disturbing the present here, hope provides an ontological security for the future.

Community futures/future imaginings

As the Riverland emerged from conditions of drought and the emphasis on crisis dissipated, there was space to consider what community futures might look like. Interestingly, water for irrigation was absent in these narratives about the future. Irrigators spoke about economic development of the community through tourism, building the Riverland, and keeping young people in their communities or otherwise, but discussions about the future never appeared fully formed. Instead, they were presented primarily as abstract musings given the 'intangibility of time' and especially the future (Grosz, 1999, p. 1). Optimism for the future of horticulture and the Renmark community was also tempered by an uncertainty about what future developments might be possible to bring wealth to the community. An irrigator explained:

> Everyone's looking for the next big thing ... but it might not come from the land. It could be tourism; it could be as a retirement centre ... nobody knows and nobody's investing.

Questions about how to develop Renmark were commonly repeated among participants. Most often, the answers were economically based speculations grounded in *past* understandings of what the future might be. For many, considerations of the future relied upon socially reproduced forms both within and outside their own community, in particular tourism, perhaps because that has so often been the focus of regional energies when attempting to revive and/or retain communities (e.g. Alonso and Northcote, 2010; Yiannakis and Davies, 2012). As an element of leisure consumption, tourism is one of the leading industries in the world, representing over 1 trillion dollars spent annually (Campbell, 2007, p. 222). A large number of irrigators commented on this, interestingly basing tourism opportunities on the river, which suggests an assumption about the health of the water system, despite previous emergency conditions. For example:

> tourism will be a big growth industry for us, I believe, because we're still going to have that water through the system.
>
> (Irrigator)

Another participant explained:

> we've got the best water skiing country in the world here, we've got a broad, flat river, we've got a river that does lots of turns ... it's always smooth water. So for water sport we've got natural wetlands here.
>
> (Irrigator)

And another irrigator stated:

> there's always going to be a river there, then you're going to have that tourism ... tourism will be a big growth industry for us, I believe.

Narratives about the river and its potential for recreation are continued in the way the Riverland is recalled as a place of beauty and activity. As one irrigator described:

> I think the council's done a fantastic job ... when you look at the riverfront and what they've done over the years ... one lady stayed in the town, she said 'Wow, your town's beautiful' so I think the council has been really good with their development of it from the aspect of what the riverfronts like, it's got the best riverfront of any of the Riverland towns. And I guess it's still on the highway, the development of – I would imagine the development of the plaza and more importantly that Big W store, but I think that retail wise attracts a lot of people from the other towns, you've got a pool coming in, it has – we've got KFC and Macca's [McDonalds] ...
>
> (Irrigator)

The beauty of the river, its 'smooth water' and 'natural wetlands' tell of a place of respite and recreation, a place that people who do not live in Renmark would be drawn to. Thus, the future hope about water is as an aesthetic, rather than a productive source. Water for irrigation becomes absent from future imaginings, either because it is taken for granted as a continuing right, or it remains absent from fear associated with loss of property. Water and community come together to create place (see Chapter 3) that privileges a diverse or indeed, different economy. While the future imaginings of what Renmark might be capture the notion of communities in a process of becoming and that possible futures are open, they also indicate that potentially different futures remain absent. As Chapter 4 demonstrated, Indigenous communities and their knowledge of space, time and community in relation to river health and development remain unacknowledged. As Bastian (2014, p. 147) suggests, 'the future is already claimed for a particular group, thus subsuming or hiding the futures of excluded groups' or 'explicitly [denying] ... their futurity' (Bastian, 2014, p. 148). As such a more open future 'requires critical approaches to the past' (Bastian, 2014, p. 149; see also Taylor, 2013).

Conclusion

Historical connections inscribed in legislation, past water practices and embodied biographies shape the present and potential future contours of irrigation communities. Rights to water are woven into biographies past and present, reaching into the future whereby water becomes a symbol for individual rights. Water as a right requires reflexive action through litigious activity and through collective resistance to policy makers, other states and environmentalist or other community members with divergent views. Reflexive work emerges as a call to collectivity in response to what is understood as risk, a crisis. Although it may be a fractured call, in which not all individuals are equally represented, there is nevertheless a collectivity created by the need to rally to address the 'threat'. This crisis or risk is not necessarily drought but threats to reduce water allocations and changes to water practices. In the Riverland these threats are also lived as a crisis in relation to irrigators questioning their own knowledge in being able to individually divert present political contingencies. Hence, collectivity also enables access to other knowledges and practices enacted through giving trust to local organisations and in particular the water trust. Threats became more pronounced for irrigators as drought continued over time and as governments sought to further regulate to ensure water efficiencies. Collective action, then, was a present attempt to 'control' the future and collectivity became increasingly robust as threats increased.

However, as the threat of drought began to dissipate, as was seen in the Australian context, and the time of emergency eased, the influence of temporalities changed significantly, resulting in an erosion of collectivity and a shift in possible futures. Narratives were reworked from that of risk to a belief in predictable water cycles, that is, an understanding that at some point it will 'always rain'. With rain, desire and hope are infused in narratives and the present and future remain undisturbed by threat and change. Thus, certainty or tempered certainty begins to replace the uncertainty of drought. Perhaps to enable the imagining of different futures, what is needed is a move away from certainty for a period of time to a sustained space of ambivalence. The concept of ambivalence is a state whereby actors are unable to choose between alternatives and they experience disorder and through disorder, discomfort (Bauman, 1991). Therefore, an ambivalence about the future is one marked by uncertainty, anxiety and ontological insecurity. Ambivalence provides an alternative to momentarily 'fixed' futures, and as such may unlock new ways of imagining community futures. These new futures may come into being as ambivalence and may also be read as hope (Junge, 2008). Junge (2008, p. 48) argues that:

> Ambivalence forms the basis for a strong criticism of an order, a chance to emancipate from order. Thus, the reconstruction of ambivalence now constitutes the possibility to free oneself, individually or collectively, from a given order by disenchanting the order.

Hence, a state of ambivalence with the breaking of drought may provide an opportunity for hope and re-imagining of water practices. It may contribute to reduced social inequalities in access and governance of water and produce more sustainable human and non-human futures.

This chapter has demonstrated that space is also a temporal reality, and the lived experiences of those who inhabit the space at any fixed point therefore represent the culmination of not only the histories of that which has come before, but also the present moments of 'now', and the possible imaginings of the future. Hence, as Royce (1968, p. 143) suggests, 'both a community of hope and a community of memory are required elements of a community'. These elements of hope and memory, as well as practice and experience, bring the past and present into focus and traverse the future. Like the past and the present, possible future articulations for irrigation communities are always a political endeavour shaped by multiple envisionings and contestations. As Grosz (1999, p. 7) suggests, to understand potential futures we must explore the various 'ontological, epistemological, political and social implications' of time.

References

Ahmed, S., 2004. *The cultural politics of emotion*. Edinburgh: Edinburgh University Press.

Alonso, A.D. and Northcote, J., 2010. The development of olive tourism in Western Australia: a case study of an emerging tourism industry. *International Journal of Tourism Research*, 12(6), pp. 696–708.

Bakker, K., 2012. Water: political, biopolitical, material. *Social Studies of Science*, 42(4), pp. 616–623.

Bastian, M., 2014. Time and community: a scoping study. *Time and Society*, 23(2), pp. 137–166.

Bauman, Z., 1991. *Modernity and ambivalence*. Cambridge: Polity Press.
Binkley, S., 2009. Governmentality, temporality and practice from the individualization of risk to the contradictory movements of the soul. *Time and Society*, 18(1), pp. 86–105.
Brace, C. and Geoghegan, H., 2010. Human geographies of climate change: landscape, temporality, and lay knowledges. *Progress in Human Geography*, 38, pp. 476–489.
Brandth, B. and Haugen, M., 2000. From lumberjack to business manager: masculinity in the Norwegian forestry press. *Journal of Rural Studies*, 16(4), pp. 343–356.
Bryant, L., 1999. The detraditionalization of occupational identities in farming in South Australia. *Sociologia Ruralis*, 39(2), pp. 236–261.
Campbell, K., 2007. Creating the land of the sky: tourism and society in western North Carolina. *Journal of Social History*, 41(1), pp. 222–224.
Crang, M. and Travlou, P.S., 2001. The city and topologies of memory. *Environment and Planning D*, 19(2), pp. 161–178.
Deleuze, G., 1988. *Bergsonism*. New York: Zone Books.
Dunst, A. and Edwards, C., 2011. Collective subjects, emancipatory cultures and political transformation. *Subjectivity*, 4(1), pp. 1–8.
Edwards, M., 2013. Fetal death and reduced birth rates associated with exposure to lead-contaminated drinking water. *Environmental Science and Technology*, 48(1), pp. 739–746.
Gill, F., 2013. Succession planning and temporality: the influence of the past and the future. *Time and Society*, 22(1), pp. 76–91.
Green, M., 2014. Chapters 346 and 347: keeping California's thirst for groundwater in check. *McGeorge Law Review*, 46, pp. 425–437.
Gregory, D. and Urry, J., 1985. *Social relations and spatial structures*. Basingstoke: Palgrave Macmillan.
Grosz, E., 1999. *Becomings: explorations in time, memory, and futures*. Ithaca, NY: Cornell University Press.
Grosz, E.A., 2005. *Time travels*. Crows Nest, NSW: Allen and Unwin.
Haraway, D., 1988. Situated knowledges: the science question in feminism and the privilege of partial perspective. *Feminist studies*, 14(3), pp. 575–599.
Jameson, F., 1991. *Postmodernism, or, the cultural logic of late capitalism*. Durham, NC: Duke University Press.
Junge, M., 2008. Bauman on ambivalence: fully acknowledging the ambiguity of ambivalence. In: M.H. Jacobsen and P. Poder, eds, *The sociology of Zygmunt Bauman: challenges and critique*. Aldershot: Ashgate, pp. 41–56.
Kiem, A.S. and Austin, E.K., 2013. Drought and the future of rural communities: opportunities and challenges for climate change adaptation in regional Victoria, Australia. *Global Environmental Change*, 23(5), pp. 1307–1316.
Kuehne, G., 2013. My decision to sell the family farm. *Agriculture and Human Values*, 30(2), pp. 203–213.
Lefebvre, H., 1991. *The production of space*. Oxford: Blackwell.
Lombard, M., 2013. Struggling, suffering, hoping, waiting: perceptions of temporality in two informal neighbourhoods in Mexico. *Environment and Planning D: Society and Space*, 31(5), pp. 813–829.
Massey, D., 1991. A global sense of place. *Marxism Today*, June, pp. 24–29.
Massey, D., 1992. Politics and space/time. *New Left Review*, 196, pp. 65–84.
Massey, D., 2005. *For space*. London: Sage.

Miller, J., 2014. California's new sweeping groundwater regulations in High Country News. Available at: www.hcn.org/issues/46.19/californias-sweeping-new-groundwater-regulations (Accessed 20 December 2015).

Quiggin, J., 2001. Environmental economics and the Murray–Darling river system. *Australian Journal of Agricultural and Resource Economics*, 45(1), pp. 67–94.

Rose, G. and Tolia-Kelly, D.P., 2012. Introducing a manifesto for practice. In: G. Rose and D.P. Tolia-Kelly, eds, *Visuality/materiality*. Surrey: Ashgate Publishing, pp. 1–12.

Royce, J., 1968. *The problem of Christianity*. Chicago: University of Chicago Press.

Soja, E., 1989. *Postmodern geographies: the reassertion of space in critical social theory*. London: Verso.

Taylor, Y., 2013. (Dis)orientations in past, present, and future encounters. *Qualitative Inquiry*, 19(10), pp. 828–838.

Till, K.E., 2012. Wounded cities: memory-work and a place-based ethics of care. *Political Geography*, 31, pp. 3–14.

Tilley, C., 2006. Introduction: identity, place, landscape and heritage. *Journal of Material Culture*, 11(1/2), pp. 7–32.

Williams, S. and Booth, K., 2013. Time and the spatial post-politics of climate change: insights from Australia. *Political Geography*, 36, pp. 21–30.

Yiannakis, J.N. and Davies, A., 2012. Diversifying rural economies through literary tourism: a review of literary tourism in Western Australia. *Journal of Heritage Tourism*, 7(1), pp. 33–44.

7 Realms of knowing

Water, a socio-natural phenomenon, is shaped by and shapes the geopolitics of communities in a myriad of complex ways. For social and cultural geography, theorisations of 'wet geographies' have been relatively new. To date, 'wet geographies' have focused on oceans and western knowledges (e.g. Anderson and Peters, 2014; Linton, 2010; Steinberg, 1999; 2014) but few have examined rivers and groundwater in relation to communities. There is little in-depth exploration of how communities, particularly in the global north, come into being, shift and change in relation to water politics.

This book has begun an unfinished story of water and irrigation communities, unfinished because communities and water/landscapes are always in the process of becoming. Any story about water and the local will always be situated, partial, and fragmented. Thus, this text captures fragmented realms of memory and knowing in relation to the defining and redefining of drought as lived in two rural sites, one in the district of Central California and the other in the Riverland, South Australia. These communities share similarities in the produce grown and a reliance upon irrigation in arid climates, and hold economic significance for their national economies (Chapter 5).

In the theatre of water politics, both sites share a recalling of the past through the continuous telling of histories to make sense of the present circumstances of drought and needs for water allocation (Chapters 2, 3 and 4). They both show a collectivity among producers in their demands to access and own water (Chapters 4, 5 and 6). This collectivity is further forged in the way farmers perceive their place nationally in the context of nearby cities and other states who have access to the same water system. Their unity is formed from a shared position of bargaining with federal and state bodies to retain what is understood as their right to water (Chapters 5 and 6). At the same time, fracture, disenchantment, contestation and individualised modes of water practice share this theatre (Chapters 4 and 5). Historical forces and wealth shape uneven risk of weathering drought and through uneven exposure to risk, cracks in the surface of unity appear. The diversity among farmers in economic and social living conditions shapes their ability to remain viable during drought. Factors shaping viability include scale of enterprise and their physical placement along the river which determines 'first in time rights' to water access in the USA. These individualised demands for water access have been maintained through litigious action by relatively wealthier farmers and corporations. In Australia, unity is a response to threat, uncertainty and risk and during the breaking of the drought individualised understandings of water and competition between irrigators become pronounced.

Across both sites, unity has meant the unity of particular groups at particular moments in time. Contestations at the local level, around risk, threat and water occur most often where ideologies, practices and material circumstances conflict. In short, in California and in Australia debates continue between environmentalists and irrigators in relation to how much water should be used and for what purpose and whether water practices should privilege the current economy or ecological health. However, with the receding of drought in Australia, these debates appear less frequently in public forums despite the country's experiences of recurrent drought. Risk becomes revealed spatially and temporally, in relation to culture and socionatures and capital, shaping riskscapes in relation to access to and quality of water (Chapter 5).

This book has brought into focus local meanings about water, demonstrating that meanings are subject to politics within and across communities, including the politics of identity, and are open to multiple knowledges, imaginaries, practices, policies, emotions and corporeality(s). The themes of knowing and/or knowledge weave through virtually all aspects of the above-mentioned articulation of water/landscapes. As a consequence, this final chapter examines how knowledges and knowing permeate the text to configure land/waterscapes.

The knowledges and knowing of water politics

The *becoming* of irrigation communities is a hard to grasp, multifaceted, changing process informed by histories, questions of belonging, social inequalities, laws, ideologies and perhaps least of all, material flows of water. Communities come into the realm of knowing for rural peoples through both tacit knowing and articulated knowledges. Tacit knowing is 'knowledge that is inarticulate and unarticulated' (Mukerji, 2014, p. 38) and articulated knowledges are those that are discursively produced, practiced and embedded in institutional frameworks working as regimes of power (Foucault, 1980). Both forms of knowledge are situated and embodied and may work simultaneously in harmony or conflict to constitute how water and community are understood at the local level.

Realms of knowing 135

In this book hegemonic, disparate, contested and fragmented realms of knowing are recalled through memories, discourses, embodied practices and cultures, echoing their presence and absence in local meanings about water use and water politics (Chapters 3 and 4). These echoes shroud how various actors in communities engage in or are dismissed from shaping political debates about how much water, the quality of water, for whom and how it is regulated and governed.

Tacit knowing by its very nature is harder to identify than formal knowledge. Mukerji, drawing on Polyani, suggests 'tacit knowledge is about sequences, practices and transformation – not stabilized truths, but *changing* logics about what could be *done next*' (2014, p. 350, emphasis in original). This form of knowledge learnt from repetition can create competency, through a type of automatic doing, and at the same time can serve as a form of social reproduction in ways of doing. Tacit knowledge for scholars like Deleuze (1988) is far from lacking in imagination or creativity. It is practice which draws on multiple senses and examples are often provided of artisans creating with material forms something born from 'a previsualization' (Mukerji, 2014, p. 356). However, if tacit knowledge is a 'knowing' through the senses, an unarticulated knowing is also how we come to 'know' where we live. While the buildings and land/waterscapes which surround us change over time, that which we come into contact with daily remains fairly constant, reinforcing a repetitive practice of 'seeing'. We can come to know our communities, its materials and peoples in this way. Chapter 4 showed the importance of material sites in tacitly shaping images and identities in communities and questions of belonging. The building and rooms of the irrigation trust herald a patriarchal colonial past where white settlement was deeply intertwined with production and economy and therefore the need for irrigation. These spatialities erased the presence of Indigenous peoples, women and people from diverse ethnicities. They constituted a particular way of knowing that reproduced frontier imaginaries, reinforcing the control of nature and channelling of water flows for agriculture. Hence, this knowing of place reproduces hegemonic histories and is one 'where erasure and absence inform social relations as much as presence and continuity do' (Degnen, 2013, p. 554). Materiality and memory shape knowing; however, these ways of knowing are sustained by *practices* that shape ongoing exclusions and inclusions in water communities. Chapter 4 demonstrated that opportunities for women and some ethnicities in water governance in Australia and elsewhere remain restricted and that Indigenous peoples are rarely consulted about water governance and river health despite their intimate knowledge of the river ecology.

Time, knowledge, embodiment and subjectivities

Chapter 3 interrogated how water is brought into realms of knowing not necessarily through its sheer presence or absence in place but through shifting memories about water as a resource embedded in historical tensions around ownership and use for irrigation. Memory as a recalled way of knowing shapes collective identities for farmers and therefore discourses of water as a property that is owned for agricultural purposes. In Central California water access based on historical continuity since colonisation and practiced through appropriation and riparianism shape the notion of water as a right for agriculturalists. According to Mannheim (1959), memory works across temporal spaces of past and future and as such, the past gets drawn into the present and reworked into the future (see Pickering and Keightley, 2012, p. 117). The thread of continuity across past-present-future which privileges understandings of water as a means to farm situates alternate meanings as discordant and a threat to farming (Chapter 6). This knowledge of water as a means for primary production is built and reproduced from collective memories or 'form[s] of memory associated with social groups' (Poole, 2008, p. 149) shared amongst farmers. Memories and practices become preserved and reinforced as:

> We learn to remember aspects of our own past only insofar as we learn that certain public objects and practices represent a past that is common to those we are interacting with.
>
> (Poole, 2008, p. 155)

Hence, contested views challenge both the collective and memory and are perceived as a threat not only to property but also to the self. In this way, 'embodied involvement in ... [water] world[s] in which landscapes are co-fabricated' (Whatmore, 2006, p. 603) continue to mark or stick to rural bodies and subjectivities. This suggests that certain affects stick to us through what we know and what is made known to us. As Ahmed suggests:

> Not only do we read such feelings, but also how the feelings feel in the first place may be tied to past history of readings, in the sense that the process of recognition (of this feeling, or that feeling) is bound up with what we already know.
>
> (2004, p. 25)

In irrigation communities then, memory and affect shape threat in relation to what is known to us about the greater world, ourselves and our communities. For irrigators, the threat and risk of drought is embodied and known from past histories and knowledges which constitute drought as a diminishing of livelihood and a threat to ongoing viability. Technical risk management knowledges constitute drought as a threat to be managed by the self, while governmental knowledges enacted through policy and practice are understood by farmers to create a 'man-made drought' (Chapters 5 and 6). In consequence, threat in relation to water and productivity is felt as demise, an undoing of farmer subjectivities (Bryant and Garnham, 2015). For farmers, the farming property is a 'signifier of farmer subjectivity refracted through quality and age of [farming] equipment, farming practices selected and condition of the land and stock, used to evaluate perceived success or otherwise' (Bryant and Garnham, 2015, p. 70). In Australia in the Riverland dying and dried orange groves and vines visible from the roads signalled property decline and assumptions about farmers' lack of risk management practices during times of drought (Bryant and Garnham, 2013). As Bryant and Garnham (2015, p. 67) have argued, 'moralized relations of value conferred to the subjectivity of farmers ... are navigated according to an ethic of "success" or "failure" as a farmer'. Discourses of farmer masculinities are enmeshed in the subject position of 'good farmer' and neo-liberal subjecthood which evaluates success in regard to economic growth. These neo-liberal discourses value particular knowledges related to business skills and development and tacit knowledges about reading markets and potential market shifts. Together, these discursive constructions 'operate within a moral economy to confer community status to male farmers and imbue subject positions with affect' (Bryant and Garnham, 2015, p. 71). These discourses, moreover, are gendered and classed and moral worth is attributed to certain masculinities and economic circumstances, knowledges and skills associated with 'the good farmer' (Bryant and Pini, 2009). Gender and class are inscribed on irrigators' bodies, that is, 'how these bodies are made, perceived and practiced in relation to cultural values (Bryant and Garnham, 2015, p. 71) 'premised on morality, embodied in personhood and realized (or not) as property value in symbolic systems of exchange' (Skeggs, 2005, p. 969, cited in Bryant and Garnham, 2015, p. 71).

How farming bodies are constituted impacts on relationships to land, water, self and community, pointing to the interstices of multiple materialities. Thus, cultural and historic meanings about farming as an activity and land as a productive entity shape meanings about water and together these are implicated in subjectivities marking the bodies of farmers over time (Chapters 3 and 6). At this nexus, as Whatmore (2006, p. 603) argues, '"livingness" [emerges as] ... a modality of connection between bodies (including human bodies) and (geo-physical) worlds'.

Individualisation, neo-liberal knowledge of entrepreneurship: water as a right

Articulating the contexts and conditions of water and community in Fresno and Renmark shows that under neo-liberal discourses and practices, water becomes increasingly tradable and as such, a commodity (Chapters 2 and 3). The notion of water as a commodity is not in discord with discourses of water as a right (Chapter 5). Neo-liberal regimes of power underscore individualised entrepreneurial action, distinguished by competition and calculable decisions based on market assessments. Water within neo-liberal regimes is to be traded among agriculturalists to engender profit. Farmers within this system of working are both enabled and constrained as they are required to act within prescribed fields delimited by the market and governmental legislation and policies. Hence, water becomes known through individual access, responsibility and rights. Water allocation as a right directly linked to ownership of land also informs the histories of mobilisation by irrigators in relation to water allocations (Chapter 6). For irrigators in Central California and the Riverland, mobilisation occurs around risk to water rights. Risk is brought into knowing relationally, that is, in relation to those who stand outside the collective – non-irrigators, governments, environmentalists and other divergent voices; it is revealed and defined in the context of uncertainties associated with water prices and allocations (Chapters 5 and 6).

In relation to governments, drought is constructed as a risk and made known to rural communities predominantly through declarations that water is in short supply and will be rationed accordingly. As Herbert-Cheshire and Higgins (2004, p. 293) suggest, 'particular "truths" about the risks facing rural communities are constructed and normalised in such a way that certain risk management techniques become self-evident'. In the context of drought, the knowledge terrain of 'risk management' comes to the fore, with the expectation that irrigators will undertake various steps to manage for recurrent droughts (Chapter 5). Risk becomes known as a destabilising phenomenon to be controlled procedurally (Neisser, 2014). Understanding risk and drought as a natural problem to be managed provides reductive understandings of water, confining its meaning to the realms of productivity and economy. It is at the juncture of economy and society that what constitutes the purpose of water is most obviously contained within the milieus of politics. Political ecology or the 'political economy of environmental change' (Bakker, 2003, p. 36) brings into focus the role of states and capital in shaping understandings of and practices associated with water (Chapter 5). Risks and uncertainty associated with water access become unequal and dependent on the power inherent in the centralisation and concentration of capital. In consequence, riskscapes are uneven, embodied and lived. The 'burden of mitigation' (Balazs and Ray, 2011, p. 607) is inequitable, with households, particularly poor Hispanic households in Central California, having to negotiate with authorities for healthy drinking water, water free from excessive nitrates and arsenic. Furthermore, irrigators with smaller properties in the Riverland and in the USA bear proportionally greater risk associated with farm continuance. Riskscapes therefore bring into being knowledges that shape an embodied reality of the complex ways in which water is a socio-cultural phenomenon.

Futures: known and unknown

In part, community futures are about what is unknown but also come into being from past and present ways of knowing. The multiple possibilities for community futures that emerge in this book are an amalgam of the past and present understandings of water rights as outlined in legislation, water governance and water policies and practices. Overall, as drought appears to breed threat, community members understood a sustainable future as one where the present is controlled. In order to control the present and potentially the future, most participants, including irrigators, journalists and lobbyists, focused on the need for governments to change how water is allocated (Chapters 5 and 6). Water allocation was the pinnacle for the unfolding and folding (Deleuze, 1988, p. 55) of futures, despite divergent political positions around water rights.

However, as Chapter 6 demonstrated, community futures are not a simple rehearsing of the past into the future but also include future imaginings. In drought, when under threat, hope for the future is somewhat repressed but has not subsided entirely. The narratives of irrigators told of an emergent hope, whereby a future was visible but could not be easily articulated. Some irrigators reported a sense of knowing that the community would not necessarily decline but there would be financial, natural and social pain. As one irrigator said, 'my gut feeling is that the Riverland is not going to be in a good state'. Others drew on their knowledges of community development enacted in other nearby towns where new economic activities were introduced like tourism, thereby envisioning a future of economic sustainability that does not rely on agriculture. Agriculture, however, was not seen to be in demise. Tacit knowledges learnt and lived through the repetition of the cyclical nature of agricultural economies shaped visions of the future as either uncertain or as requiring new practices. Whether new practices were foreseen was dependent on eco-political views that promoted change to water practices to enable healthier river systems. Those who invested in change to water practices had a particular temporal understanding of hope, that is, a position where 'hope requires that we must act in the present, rather than simply wait for a future that is always before us' (Ahmed, 2004, p. 184).

In concluding this book we argue that water is a political subject just as community is a political subject. However, irrigation communities are more than the sum of water, land and community and are separately and collectively 'contested, worked and reworked' (Tilley, 2006, p. 7). The narratives of drought, the breaking of drought and past-present-futures of irrigation communities show that communities are always in flux. They are always in a state of becoming and in this way, are not quite knowable. However, what is revealed about irrigation communities through the case studies of Central California and South Australia is that they are shaped by realms of knowledges and ways of knowing that shape water practices and diverse aspects of social life including identities, belonging, economies and social practices. Indeed, these places are 'palimpsests of past and present ... and are understood in relation to differing social and political agendas' (Tilley, 2006, p. 8). At the local level, such agendas are revealed through:

> set[s] of practices of how people position themselves in multiple ways within overlapping webs of relations; relations with people, relations with places, relations with memory, relations with change and relations with the past.
>
> (Degnen, 2013, p. 554)

In addition and importantly, analyses of ways of knowing within and beyond irrigation communities bring to light relations with materiality and materialism. The politics of water and community is a politics associated with relational definitions of both water and land and how each is understood in the context of the other – it is a politics that centralises materialism and capital. The becoming of irrigation communities is a spatial and temporal becoming – a fusion of social, natural, economic, political and cultural relations filled with possibilities. These possibilities can enable alternative community futures which need not reproduce inequalities and uneven risks to subjects and to the water and land from which irrigation communities spring.

References

Ahmed, S., 2004. *The cultural politics of emotion*. Edinburgh: Edinburgh University Press.

Anderson, J. and Peters, K., eds., 2014. *Water worlds: human geographies of the ocean*. Surrey: Ashgate Publishing.

Bakker, K., 2003. A political ecology of water privatization. *Studies in Political Economy*, 70(Spring), pp. 35–57.

Balazs, C.L. and Ray, I., 2014. The drinking water disparities framework: on the origins and persistence of inequities in exposure. *American Journal of Public Health*, 104(4), pp. 603–611.

Bryant, L. and Garnham, B., 2013. Beyond discourses of drought: the micro-politics of the wine industry and farmer distress. *Journal of Rural Studies*, 32, pp. 1–9.

Bryant, L. and Garnham, B., 2015. The fallen hero: masculinity, shame and farmer suicide in Australia. *Gender, Place and Culture*, 22(1), pp. 67–82.

Bryant, L. and Pini, B., 2009. Gender, class and rurality: Australian case studies. *Journal of Rural Studies*, 25(1), pp. 48–56.

Degnen, C., 2013. 'Knowing', absence, and presence: the spatial and temporal depth of relations. *Environment and Planning D: Society and Space*, 31, pp. 554–570.

Deleuze, G., 1988. *Bergsonism*. New York: Zone Books.
Foucault, M., 1980. Two lectures. In: C. Gordon, ed., *Power/knowledge: selected interviews and other writing by Michel Foucault, 1972–1977*. New York: Pantheon, pp. 78–108.
Herbert-Cheshire, L. and Higgins, V., 2004. From risky to responsible: expert knowledge and the governing of community-led rural development. *Journal of Rural Studies*, 20(3), pp. 289–302.
Linton, J., 2010. *What is water? The history of a modern abstraction*. Vancouver: University of British Columbia Press.
Mannheim, K., 1959. *Ideology and utopia: an introduction to the sociology of knowledge*. New York: Harcourt, Brace.
Mukerji, C., 2014. The cultural power of tacit knowledge: inarticulacy and Bourdieu's habitus. *American Journal of Cultural Sociology*, 2(3), pp. 348–375.
Pickering, M. and Keightley, E., 2012. Communities of memory and the problem of transmission. *European Journal of Cultural Studies*, 16(1), pp. 115–131.
Poole, R., 2008. Memory, history and the claims of the past. *Memory Studies*, 1(2), pp. 149–166.
Steinberg, P.E., 1999. Navigating to multiple horizons: toward a geography of ocean-space. *The Professional Geographer*, 51(3), pp. 366–375.
Steinberg, P.E., 2014. Mediterranean metaphors: travel, translation and oceanic imaginaries in the 'new mediterraneans' of the Arctic Ocean, the Gulf of Mexico and the Caribbean. In: J. Anderson and K. Peters, eds, *Water worlds: human geographies of the ocean*. Surrey: Ashgate Publishing, pp. 23–38.
Tilley, C., 2006. Introduction: identity, place, landscape and heritage. *Journal of Material Culture*, 11(1/2), pp. 7–32.
Whatmore, S., 2006. Materialist returns: practicing cultural geography in and for a more-than-human world. *Cultural Geographies*, 13(4), pp. 600–609.

Index

A reference in *italics* refers to a figure.

Actor Network Theory (ANT) 89, 90
Adam, B. and Van Loon. J. 88–9
advertising: household water reduction campaigns 2, *3*; roadside protest signs, Fresno 121–3, *121*, *122*
affect 69–70, 136
agriculture: discourse of economics in 49–50; emotional attachment to material sites (farms) 54; family succession patterns 53–5; farming bodies 137; in Fresno 17, 50–1, 102; in Riverland 14; settlement narratives and 74–5, 100; subjectivities of farmers 137; women's role in 71
Agyeman, J. and Spooner, R. 61
Ahlers, R. and Zwarteveen, M. 68, 71
Ahmed, S. 136
Albrecht et al. (2007) 49
Alkon, A.H. and Traugot, M. 44
Alston, M. and Mason, R. 72
Anderson, B. 70
Anderson, J. and Peters, K. 11
Anderson et al. (2006) 64, 65
Askins, K. 9, 77, 78
Association of California Water Agencies (ACWA) 35, 36
Australia: annual rulings on water allocations 4; dominance of settler imaginaries 73–4; drought relief programs 104; map of Southeastern region *15*; Native Title 75; rural spaces as multi-cultural 61, 77, 78–9; *see also* Renmark, Riverland; Riverland, South Australia

Bachmann, R. and Zaheer, A. 90
Bakker, K. 10
Balazs, C.L. and Ray, I. 96–7
Bastian, M. 113
Beck, G. and Kropp, C. 90
Beck, U. 88, 90
Bender, B. 12, 63–4
Berger, J. and Mohr, J. 43–4
Binkley, S. 119, 125
Bjornlund et al. (2010) 93
bodies: affect and 69–70; body and nature experiences 8–9; discomfort of place 69–70, 77; farming bodies 137; gendered discomfort 70; and riskscapes 87
Boxall, B. 104
Bratspies, R.M. 93
Brown, Jerry 2, 36, 116
Bryant, L. and Garnham, B. 14, 74, 94, 137
Bryant, L. and George, J. 13, 91, 93, 95
Bryant, L. and Jaworski, K. 72–3
Bryant, L. and Livholts, M. 66

Index

Bryant, L. and Pini, B. 74
built environment: exclusion/belonging dynamics and 79; impact of immigration on 77, 78–9

California: appropriative rights 32, 102; complex water policies 31, 102; conflicts around water rights 102–3; diversity of terrain 32; drought State of Emergency 2; Gold Rush 32, 33; individualisation and water rights 101–2; large-scale projects, California 34–5; non-sustainable situation 37; riparian rights 32, 33, 101; 'Save Our Water Campaign' 2, *3*; as settler society 33; 2014 Groundwater Regulation Act 116–17; water control mechanisms, California 34–6; water policies, overview of 33–4; *see also* Central California; Fresno; groundwater, California
Carter, J. and Hollinsworth, D. 75–6
Castree, N. 99
Central California: advocacy for water rights 95, 96; commodification of water 49–50, 137–8; drought and new water policies 120–1; environmental vs. economic concerns 95–6, 123–4; groundwater extraction 32, 35, 115–17; individualisation of water rights 32, 101–2, 106–7; irrigators' historical narratives 117; irrigators lack of trust in the state 103–5, 107; litigation over water rights 33–4, 102–3, 117–18, 134; protests about water allocations *4*; risk amelioration mechanisms 92–3; state water infrastructure 96, 124; water quality and contamination 96–100; *see also* Fresno
Central Valley Project 34
Chaffey brothers 9, 25, 72, 73, 74, 77
climate change: environmental challenges, Murray-Darling Basin 14–15; as future threat 114

collective memory: and connection to place 43; constructed nature of 42; fractures in, Fresno 52; and imagined communities 42; and individual memory 42–3; irrigation as multi-generational act 53–5; and memorials 64; and place-making 44; as social activity 43; *see also* memory
colonial narratives: patriarchal colonial past of RIT building 60–1, 68, *69*; and place-making 45; of Renmark's past 74; and social relations 5; and transrural experiences 10
communities: centrality of Murray River, Riverland 8, 46–9; collective memory and community building 42–3; community futures and collective actions, Riverland 118–20, 133–4; community tensions over water policy, Central California 52, 123–4; continuity and family succession trends 53–5; effects of risk on 90; imagined communities 42; impact of end of drought, Renmark 125–6; meanings of 4–5; past-present knowledge and community futures 139–40; shared ethical positions and risk 94–5; time-space dynamic and 113; trust in the collective, Fresno 96, 133; *see also* rural communities
Council of Australian Governments (CoAG) reforms 27
Crang, M. and Travlou, P.S. 113
cultural geography 99
culture/nature relationship 6, 7–9
Cummins, T. and Watson, A. 24, 30

Davidson, J. and Milligan, C. 47
Degnen, C. 140
Deleuze, G. 114, 135
Derrien, M.M. and Stokowski, P.A. 45
drought: community effects of, Riverland 48–9; definition, USA 2;

144 *Index*

drought relief programs 104; emotional distress of 48–9; end of and pre-reflexive practices 125; future imaginings, post-drought Renmark 125–9; pragmatic decision-making and, Fresno 50–1; as risk to be managed 138; as social event 31; State of Emergency, California 2; and water policies, Central California 120–1; water scarcity in urban areas 2–3; within white Australian narratives 74
Dunst, A. and Edwards, C. 118

Edwards et al. (2008) 56
Elsner, J. 42
embodiment: and envisioning 65–6; feelings of risk 94–5, 136–7; situated embodiment 7, 62; vision and the embodied researcher 67
emotions: drought as emotional distress 48–9; effects of change on (solastalgia) 49; experiences of risk 87–8, 94–5; links to material sites 54; role in place-making 47–8; and water rights, California 102
environmental degradation: early concerns, Australia 26; vs. economic development 95–6, 123–4; and the Murray-Darling Basin 14–15, 26; water caps 27; water quality and contamination, Central California 96–8
environmental justice 98–9

feminist scholarship: landscape theories 6–7; on water 71; on water governance 72
Fitchen, J.M. 101, 103
Foucault, M. 91–2, 100
Fresno: agriculture in 17, 50–1, 102; groundwater as primary water source 16–17; Groundwater Sustainability Plan (GSP) 36–7; history of water legislation development 50; labour relations 52; pragmatic relationship with water 50–1; roadside protest signs against reduced water allocations 121–3, *121*, *122*; state subsidies to 104; trust in the collective 96, 133; *see also* California; Central California
Fresno Irrigation District 16
Fukuyama, F. 91
futures: ambivalence over 129–30; community futures and collective actions, Riverland 118–20, 133–4; future imaginings, post-drought Renmark 112–13, 125–9; inequalities of representations 114; irrigator protests and, Fresno 123; past and present ways of knowing 139–40; past-present-future configurations 113–14

Gale et al. (2014) 28–9
the gaze 62, 65
Geismar, H. and Horst, H.A. 62, 63
gender: farmer masculinities 137; gendered physical discomfort 70; and water relations 71–3; *see also* women
Giddens, T. 88
Gill, F. 53
globalisation: critiques of 9; of professional irrigation engineers 72
governmentality 91–2
Grantham, T.E. and Viers, J.H. 35
Green, M. 116
Grosz, E.A. 113, 114–15
groundwater, California: extraction of 16–17, 32, 35, 115–17; Groundwater Regulation Act 116–17; Groundwater Sustainability Plan (GSP) 36–7; Sustainable Groundwater Management Act (SGMA) 36

Halbwachs, M. 42, 43
Hall, M. 66
Hanak et al. (2011) 31, 32, 33, 34–5

Haraway, D. 62, 67, 123
Herbert-Cheshire, L. and Higgins, V. 138
Higgins, V. 90–1
Hoelscher, S. and Alderman, D.H. 43, 44
Holloway, S. 78
Hoskins, B.J. 64
Hundley, Jr N. 33

identity: and collective memory 42–3; and familial farming histories 117; politics of identity 8; rural spaces and indigenous identities 61, 75
imagined communities 42
Indigenous peoples: art 1; erasure of their pasts 61, 73–4; impact of drought 74–5; Indigenous knowledge 76, 89; Native Title 75; in the Riverland area 74; rural spaces and Indigenous identities 61, 75; stakes in water policy 75–6
individualisation: and increased water flows 101; and risk 100, 106–7, 119; settler imaginaries 100, 107; and water access 100–1; of water management 26–7; and water rights, Central California 32, 101–2, 106–7, 114
infrastructure development: large-scale projects, California 34–5; Pine Flat Dam, California 34; Riverland 25–6, 29; state/federal control over 36
institutional trust 91
institutions: and amelioration of irrigators' risk 92; and governmentality of risk 91–2; irrigators' lack of trust in government 103–4; regulatory trust in 91–2, 93; state regulation and lack of local knowledge 104–5; *see also* Renmark Irrigation Trust (RIT)
irrigation: and commodification of water 50–1; development of, historical 9–10; early settler expectations 24–5; environmental challenges to, Murray-Darling Basin 14–15, 26; impact of drought 4; from the Kings River 16–17; as male space 71, 72; and nation-building 25–6, 73–4; in Riverland 14; use of groundwater 32

Jordan et al. (2009) 77, 78–9
Junge, M. 130

Kearns, R. and Collins, D. 48
Kings River 16–17
knowing: and collective memory 42–3; and memory 136; past-present knowledge and community futures 139–40; perspectives on drought responses 26–7; tacit knowing 134, 135
knowledge: articulated knowledge 134; Indigenous knowledge 76, 89; lack of local knowledge and state regulation 104–5; and power relations 91–2; and risk 89, 93–4, 136–7; tacit knowledge 135
Krieger, L.M. 32
Kuehne, G. 117

Lahiri-Dutt, K. 12
landscape: and centering of terra 11–12; conceptualisations of 5–6; cultural understandings of 6; as external and static 6; Indigenous peoples' connection with 75; land/waterscapes 11; relationality of nature and culture 7–9; social construction of 43–4; and temporality 112
landscape art 6
landscape theories 5–13
laws: Irrigation Act 1886 (Vic.) 25; *Katz v Walkinshaw* (Cal.) 33–4; *Lux v. Haggin* 1886 33; Sustainable Groundwater Management Act (SGMA) 36; 2014 Groundwater

146 *Index*

Regulation Act 116–17; Water Act 1905 (Cth) 25; Water Act 2007 (Cth) 28; Water Amendment Act 2008 (Cth) 28; Wright Act 1887 33
legislation: Indigenous rights to water 76; individualisation in US water legislation 32, 101–2, 106–7, 114; recognition of appropriative rights 32; recognition of riparian rights 32, 33
Linton, J. 10–11
Little, J. 78
Lombard, M. 113
Luhmann, N. 106

Mannheim, K. 136
Mason, J. and Davies, K. 67
Massey, D. 5, 7, 8, 77, 112
materialism 63
materiality: agency of objects 64–5; concept of 63; emotional attachment to material sites (farms) 54; material/social relationship 62, 63–5, 99–100; and place-making 44; politics/matter relationship 64, 70; and power 66; relationality and 65; and research engagement 62; and visuality 65–6
McKay, J. 27
memory: individual/collective relationship 42–3; and knowing 136; and memorials 64; past-present-future configurations and 114; sites of memory 44, 60–1; threat to temporal notions of 53; *see also* collective memory
methodology 13–14
Möllering, G. 91
Moore et al. (2014) 23
moral discourses 2–3
Morant, Harry 'Breaker' 69
Mukerji, C. 135
Müller-Mahn, D. 89–90
Murray–Darling Basin Authority (MDBA) 28

Murray–Darling Basin Commission (MDBC) 27
Murray-Darling Basin (MDB): cap arrangements 27; environmental challenges to 14–15; impacts of water markets 56; and irrigation supply 14; map *15*; protests about water allocations 4; women on the governance board 72; *see also* Renmark, Riverland
Murray-Darling Basin Plan (MDBP): development of 27, 28; economic and social impacts of 28–9; Renmark Irrigation Trust response to 29; support for 93
Musgrave, W. 24

National Water Initiative (NWI) 27–8
nation-building 25–6
nature: and bodily experiences 8–9; culture/nature relationship 6, 7–9; engagement with man-made objects 63–4; as ever changing 7–8; relational approach to 8–9, 99; risk to and economic development 96
neo-liberalism: and commodification of water 49–51, 137–8; water governance, Riverland 26–7
non-representational theories 7–8, 65
Nora, Pierre 44
November, V. 90

Panelli et al. (2009) 77
Pini, B. 71
Pink, B. 67
place: emotional attachment to material sites (farms) 54; historical narratives of 4; as an ongoing production 5
place-making: centrality of water to 45–8; disconnection from, Fresno 52; immigration and rural communities 77–9; naming and 44; narratives of 45, 46–8; role of emotions 47–8; storytelling and

44–5; through collective memory 44; time-space factors and 113
Plummer, B. 31
political ecology 96, 138
political processes: embodied politics of envisioning 65–6; national/local interstices 5; politics/matter relationship 64, 70
Poole, R. 136
pre-reflexive practices 125
Price, L. and Evans, N. 94
Probyn, E. 47
Prout, S. and Howitt, R. 74

regulatory trust: irrigators lack of trust in the state 103–6; and local knowledge 104–5; and regulating bodies 91–2
Renmark, Riverland: built landscape 77; colonial heritage 74; community futures and collective actions 118–20, 133–4; erasure of Indigenous presence 61, 73–4; familial histories 117; future imaginings, post-drought 125–9; future tourism opportunities 127–8; settler narratives 74, 118; *see also* Murray-Darling Basin
Renmark Irrigation Trust (RIT): centralisation of water control 25; irrigators' trust in 93–5; membership of 13; over-allocation to neighbouring states 30; regulatory trust in 93; response to the Murray-Darling Basin Plan 29; tensions with individualised water access 100–1; variable exclusion of others 78–9; water pricing and allocation advocacy 93–5, 107, 119
Renmark Irrigation Trust (RIT) building: boardroom 68, *70*; boardroom as male space 69–70, 72–3, 77; patriarchal colonial past of 60–1, 68, *69*; socio-political importance of 60

rights-based discourses 4, 115–17
risk: as actant 90, 106; Actor Network Theory (ANT) 89, 90; advocacy and limited knowledge 93–4; climate change as future threat 114; as embodied 94–5, 136–7; emotional aspect to 87–8, 94–5; environmental vs. economic concerns 95–6, 123–4; governmentality of 91–2; and individualisation 100, 106–7, 119; institutional trust 91; irrigators' risk amelioration 92, 138; knowledge and 89, 90–1; in late modernity 88–9; perceived risk 90; pre-reflexive dimension 119; relational risk 92, 106–7; and space 89; and trust 90–1; water allocation and capital, Central California 95–6; water quality and contamination, Central California 96–100
riskscapes: concept of 87–8, 89–90, 107–8; human and non-human interactions in 96–100; political nature of 94, 138–9
River Murray: community dependence on water flow 14, 46–9; Indigenous meanings of 76; as lifeblood 46–8
Riverland, South Australia: centrality of water to sense of place 8, 46–8; changing water governance 28–30; and colonial settlement 24; community dependence on water flow 46–9; fruit production 14; Indigenous peoples 74; individualised water access 100–1; infrastructure development 25–6, 29; irrigation 14; irrigators lack of trust in government 103, 104, 105–6; neo-liberal water governance 26–7; risk for irrigators 93; water allocation cuts 28–9; *see also* Murray–Darling Basin (MDB); Renmark
Rose, G. 7
Rose, G. and Tolia-Kelly, D.P. 60, 65, 66, 67, 70

rural communities: absence of Indigenous narratives 61, 73–4; individualisation of water management 26–7; as multi-cultural 61, 77–9; perception of as 'white' spaces 61, 76–7; rurality of Indigenous peoples 74–6

Said, Edward 43
Sauer, C.O. 6
the senses: sensory impacts of place 67; use of photographs 67, 68
settler imaginaries: agriculture and 74–5, 100; in Australia 73–4, 118; of California 33; dominance of, rural settings 10; and individualisation 100, 107
Shaw et al. (2006) 75
sites of memory 44, 60–1
situated embodiment 7, 62
social history 7
solastalgia 49
Steinberg, P.E. 11
Szersznski, B. 89

Taylor, Y. 114
temporality: communities and time-space dynamic 113; critical temporalities 114; cyclical understandings of, post-drought Renmark 125–7; erasure of Indigenous pasts 61, 73–4; and landscape 112; as politicised 112, 114; temporal water flows 8; temporality of landscapes 7–8; threat to temporal notions of memory 53
Tilley, C. 8, 12, 60, 64, 66
transnational, term 9
transrurality: dominance of settler imaginaries 10; term 9, 77; *see also* rural communities
trust: in the collective, Fresno 96, 133; and governmentality of risk 91–2; institutional trust 91; lack of in regulatory bodies 103–4; regulatory trust 91; and risk 90–1
Tuan, Y. 44

Van Patten, S. and Williams, D. 48
Vannini. P. and Taggart, J. 11
vision: co-constitution of visuality and materiality 70; and the embodied researcher 67; politics of envisioning 65–6
visuality/materiality approach 65–6

Wallis et al. (2013) 30
water: as a feminist issue 71–2; hegemonic meanings of 10–11; as personal product 124–5; socio-cultural significance of 1; understandings of 11
water allocations: annual rulings on 4; and centralisation of capital, Central California 95–6; cuts to 28–9; inter-state competition for, Australia 30, 119–20; from the Kings River 16–17; Renmark Irrigation Trust (RIT) advocacy for 93–5, 107, 119; and rights-based discourses, California 115–17; trading of 26; uncertainty over and risk 93; and water politics 87; *see also* water policies
water flows: emotional responses to 47–9; increased and individualisation 101; pragmatic responses to 50–1
water policies: in California 32–4; for the common good, Renmark 119; community tensions over, Central California 124; complexity of, California 31, 102; and drought, Central California 120–1; early development, Australia 24–5; Indigenous rights to water 75–6; infrastructure development 25–6, 29; lack of women's representation in 71–3; and nation-building 25–6,

31, 73–4; neo-liberal water governance 26–7; non-sustainable situation, California 37; prioritisation of economic sustainability 27–8; public control, California 34; reform era, Australia 26–8; roadside protest signs against, Fresno 121–3, *121*, *122*; water control mechanisms, California 34–6; water governance as male domain 71–3; *see also* water allocations

water politics: California's water system 31; commodification of water 49–51, 137–8; fragmentation of, Central California 96; inclusion/exclusion from 61–2; Indigenous peoples, absence of 80; role of trust 90; and water allocations 87; as white, male space 80; women, absence of 71–2, 80

water pricing 93

water rights: advocacy for, Central California 95, 96; appropriative rights 32, 102; Indigenous rights to water 75–6; and individualisation, Central California 32, 101–2, 106–7, 114; and litigation, Central California 33–4, 102–3, 117–18, 134; rights-based discourses 4, 115–17; riparian rights 32, 33, 101

wet geographies 11, 133

Whatmore, S. 8, 99, 136

Wheeler et al. (2014) 54

women: in agri-political spaces 71–3; exclusion from agri-political life 61; role in agriculture 71; water as feminist issue 71; *see also* gender

Worster, D. 50

Zwarteveen, M. 72

Taylor & Francis eBooks

Helping you to choose the right eBooks for your Library

Add Routledge titles to your library's digital collection today. Taylor and Francis ebooks contains over 50,000 titles in the Humanities, Social Sciences, Behavioural Sciences, Built Environment and Law.

Choose from a range of subject packages or create your own!

Benefits for you
- Free MARC records
- COUNTER-compliant usage statistics
- Flexible purchase and pricing options
- All titles DRM-free.

Benefits for your user
- Off-site, anytime access via Athens or referring URL
- Print or copy pages or chapters
- Full content search
- Bookmark, highlight and annotate text
- Access to thousands of pages of quality research at the click of a button.

REQUEST YOUR FREE INSTITUTIONAL TRIAL TODAY

Free Trials Available
We offer free trials to qualifying academic, corporate and government customers.

eCollections – Choose from over 30 subject eCollections, including:

Archaeology	Language Learning
Architecture	Law
Asian Studies	Literature
Business & Management	Media & Communication
Classical Studies	Middle East Studies
Construction	Music
Creative & Media Arts	Philosophy
Criminology & Criminal Justice	Planning
Economics	Politics
Education	Psychology & Mental Health
Energy	Religion
Engineering	Security
English Language & Linguistics	Social Work
Environment & Sustainability	Sociology
Geography	Sport
Health Studies	Theatre & Performance
History	Tourism, Hospitality & Events

For more information, pricing enquiries or to order a free trial, please contact your local sales team:
www.tandfebooks.com/page/sales

 Routledge Taylor & Francis Group | The home of Routledge books | **www.tandfebooks.com**

Printed in the United States
By Bookmasters